REVISE BTEC NATIONAL

Business

UNIT 3

PRACTICE ASSESSMENTS Plus+

Series Consultant: Harry Smith
Author: Stephen Jakubowski

A note from the publisher

These practice assessments are designed to complement your revision and to help prepare you for the external assessment. They do not include all the content and skills needed for the complete course and have been written to help you practise what you have learned. They may not be representative of a real assessment.

While the publishers have made every attempt to ensure that advice on the qualification and its assessment is accurate, the official specification and associated assessment guidance materials are the only authoritative source of information and should always be referred to for definitive guidance.

This qualification is reviewed on a regular basis and may be updated in the future. Any such updates that affect the content of this book will be outlined at **www.pearsonfe.co.uk/BTECchanges**.

Published by Pearson Education Limited, 80 Strand, London, WC2R 0RL.

www.pearsonschoolsandfecolleges.co.uk

Typeset, produced and illustrated by QBS Ltd
Cover illustration by Miriam Sturdee

First published 2018

21 20 19 18
10 9 8 7 6 5 4 3 2 1

British Library Cataloguing in Publication Data

A catalogue record for this book is available from the British Library

ISBN 978 1 292 25667 2

Notes from the publisher

1. While the publishers have made every attempt to ensure that advice on the qualification and its assessment is accurate, the official specification and associated assessment guidance materials are the only authoritative source of information and should always be referred to for definitive guidance.

Pearson examiners have not contributed to any sections in this resource relevant to examination papers for which they have responsibility.

2. Pearson has robust editorial processes, including answer and fact checks, to ensure the accuracy of the content in this publication, and every effort is made to ensure this publication is free of errors. We are, however, only human, and occasionally errors do occur. Pearson is not liable for any misunderstandings that arise as a result of errors in this publication, but it is our priority to ensure that the content is accurate. If you spot an error, please do contact us at resourcescorrections@pearson.com so we can make sure it is corrected.

Websites

Pearson Education Limited is not responsible for the content of any external internet sites. It is essential for tutors to preview each website before using it in class so as to ensure that the URL is still accurate, relevant and appropriate. We suggest that tutors bookmark useful websites and consider enabling students to access them through the school/college intranet.

Introduction

This book has been designed to help you to practise the skills you may need for the external assessment of BTEC National Business Unit 3. You may be studying this unit as part of the BTEC National Extended Certificate, Foundation Diploma, Diploma or Extended Diploma.

About the practice assessments

The book contains four practice assessments for the unit. Unlike your actual assessment, each question has targeted hints, guidance and support in the margin to help you understand how to tackle them.

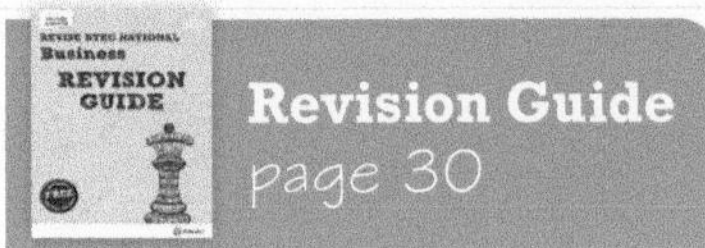

gives you links to relevant pages in the Pearson Revise BTEC National Business Revision Guide so you can revise the essential content. This will also help you to understand how the essential content is applied to different contexts when assessed.

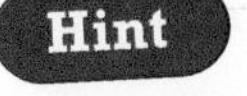

to get you started and remind you of the skills or knowledge you need to apply.

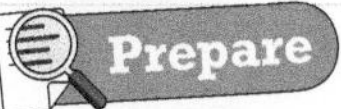

to help you on how to approach a question, such as making a brief plan.

to provide content that you need to learn such as a definition, rule or formula.

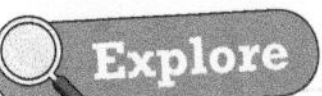

to remind you of content related to the question to aid your revision on that topic.

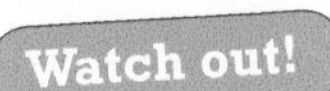

to help you avoid common pitfalls.

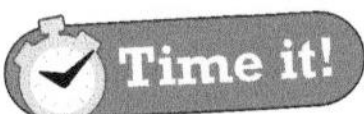

for use with the final practice assessment to help you become familiar with answering in a given time and ways to think about allocating time for different kinds of questions.

There is space for you to write your answers to the questions within this book. However, if you are carrying out research or writing notes, or simply require more space to complete your answers, you may want to use separate paper.

There is also an answer section at the back of the book, so you can check your answers for each practice assessment.

Check the Pearson website

For overarching guidance on the official assessment outcomes and key terms used in your assessment, please refer to the specification on the Pearson website. For this unit, check whether you must have a calculator in your assessment.

The practice questions, support and answers in this book are provided to help you to revise the essential content in the specification, along with ways of applying your skills. The details of your actual assessment may change, so always make sure you are up to date on its format and requirements by asking your tutor or checking the Pearson website for the most up-to-date Sample Assessment Material, Mark Schemes and any past papers.

Contents

Practice assessment 1

SECTION A: Personal Finance

Answer ALL questions.
Write your answers in the spaces provided.

Banks offer their customers a range of accounts to meet different requirements, spending habits and lifestyles. These are subject to regulation.

Give **two** types of current account.

1 ....

....

2 ....

....

Total for Question 1 = 2 marks

Revision Guide page 50

Hint

The external assessment is divided into two sections. Section A is about **Personal Finance**. Section B is about **Business Finance**. In your actual assessment, notice how long you are advised to spend on each section.

Hint

When answering this **give** question, you only need to recall types of current account. You don't need to go into detail on these types of questions. Only give the required number of responses.

Explore

Banks offer a range of different accounts to meet the financial circumstances and requirements of different customers. Some customers are willing to pay for additional banking services. Make sure you know the types, features, advantages and disadvantages, and services offered by current accounts.

Revision Guide page 57

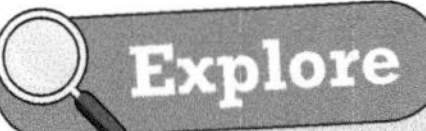

For this **describe** question, answer with a main point, then develop the point. For example: The FSCS covers claims against businesses authorised by the Financial Conduct Authority (FCA). Describe another role with a main point, then develop the point.

Explore

Make sure you can describe the role, functions and responsibilities of other organisations that protect the consumer when purchasing financial products from banks and insurance companies:

- Financial Conduct Authority (FCA) who regulate the conduct of financial service providers.
- Financial Ombudsman Service (FOS) who consumers can turn to if complaints about providers are unresolved.

2 Describe the role of the Financial Services Compensation Scheme (FSCS).

....

....

....

....

Total for Question 2 = 2 marks

3 Explain **two** ways an increase in interest rates may affect a person's spending habits.

1 ....

....

....

....

2 ....

....

....

....

Total for Question 3 = 4 marks

Revision Guide page 46

Hint

When you **explain** you give clear details and reasons, and show your understanding. For each way you provide, **first** identify an impact of an increase in interest rates, **then** give a linked reason for the effect on a person's spending habits.

Hint

A rate of interest is a **reward** for saving and a **cost** of borrowing. Consider how an increase in interest rates might encourage people to save, and how the cost of borrowing might discourage people from taking out loans.

Explore

Explain how a **reduction** in interest rates may affect a person's spending habits. For example: when interest rates are reduced, it is easier to borrow money, which can result in increased consumer spending and increases in prices.

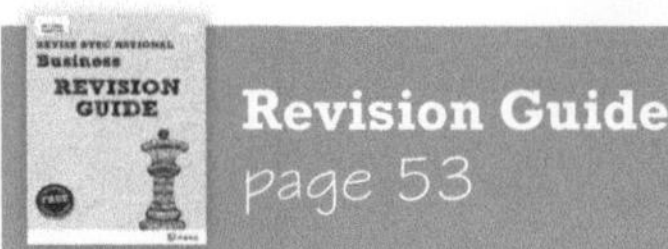
Revision Guide page 53

Hint

For this **discuss** question, think about the different aspects that Temi should consider. Consider how they link together and the extent to which they are important, giving a balanced point of view. A conclusion is not required.

Hint

The cost of insurance is known as the **premium**. The higher the risk, the higher the premium. Consider different risks covered by a travel insurance policy and factors that influence costs.

Explore

Know what is covered by, and factors that affect the cost of, other kinds of insurance:

- car – a legal requirement for owners
- home and contents – costs of rebuilding/repairs from fire or floods, for example
- life insurance and assurance – pays out money on death
- health – private medical costs; convenient treatment times
- pet – veterinary bills/illness and personal injury/damage caused by the animal.

4 Temi is planning to go on holiday to Spain after she has completed her exams and wants to know if she should purchase travel insurance.

Discuss the factors that Temi should consider when deciding whether o not to purchase travel insurance.

....

....

....

....

....

....

....

....

....

....

....

....

Total for Question 4 = 6 mark

5 The cost of university tuition fees can result in large student debts. Many parents are considering ways they can save to help support their children when they enter higher education, so they do not have to rely so much on student loans.

Assess the use of life assurance as a method of saving.

Total for Question 5 = 10 marks

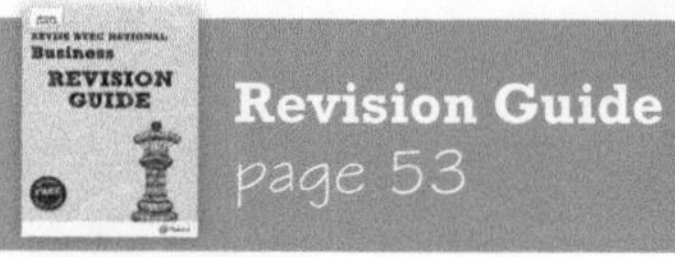

Hint

Your answer to this **assess** question should present a careful consideration of the advantages and disadvantages of life assurance as a method of saving. Your balanced assessment should lead to a conclusion.

Hint

Life **assurance** is a mixture of **life insurance** plus **investment**. Life assurance companies invest some of the premiums into shares, bonds and savings accounts.

LEARN IT!

The difference between life insurance and life assurance is that:

- with **life insurance** the policy only pays out money when the policyholder dies
- with **life assurance** the policy pays out money when the policyholder dies, but also pays a sum of money to the policyholder if they are still alive at the end of the policy term.

Revision Guide page 51

Hint

Read the **evaluate** question on the next page. You need to evaluate information about the couple and information about different mortgages, and come to a judgement about which is suitable.

Hint

Extract key factors about the couple to evaluate suitability. Circle **personal circumstances.** Underline **financial circumstances.** Star **other factors.** Decide how each one may affect the couple's mortgage decision.

Hint

To calculate the **mortgage required**, take into account the value of the property, available savings and expenses from purchasing the property.

Hint

Calculate the maximum mortgage from each lender – a multiple of joint income. Note the providers not offering the amount required as unsuitable. Evaluate the suitability of the remaining providers against personal, financial and other factors.

Watch out!

The best 'deal' for the lowest interest rate is 3% – but evaluate suitability for the client.

6 Simon and Deepa are a young couple who have been saving up to buy their first home. They currently live in rented accommodation and have no children. They have opened a joint ISA account with a deposit of £70 000. Simon is a trainee accountant with a multinational chemical company and earns £19 000; Deepa earns £25 000 as a Human Resources Manager in a local factory.
They are keen to purchase a flat in a new housing development close to the city centre. The flat is on the market for £200 000. They have appointed a solicitor who charges a fixed fee of £2000.
They have information from mortgage providers regarding deposits and interest rates. They also have the property valuation fee (a one-off, up-front fee payable to the lender).
They also have the maximum mortgage available to borrowers (this is calculated as a multiple of the income of the borrowers).

This table gives information on mortgages available from different banks and building societies.

Summary of mortgage terms and conditions

Mortgage provider	Deposit required	Interest	Mortgage period	Maximum mortgage available
Audley Building Society	10% of property valuation	3% variable	20 years	2.5 × joint income
Brimsdown Building Society	15% of property valuation	6% fixed for the first 5 years then variable	25 years	3 × joint income
Central Bank	20% of property valuation	7% fixed for the period of the mortgage	20 years	3.5 × joint income
Danesland Bank	10% of property valuation	4.75% variable	25 years	3 × joint income

Evaluate which mortgage would be most suitable for Simon and Deepa.

....

....

....

....

....

....

....

....

....

....

....

....

....

....

....

....

....

....

....

....

....

....

....

....

....

....

Total for Question 6 = 12 marks

TOTAL FOR SECTION A = 36 MARKS

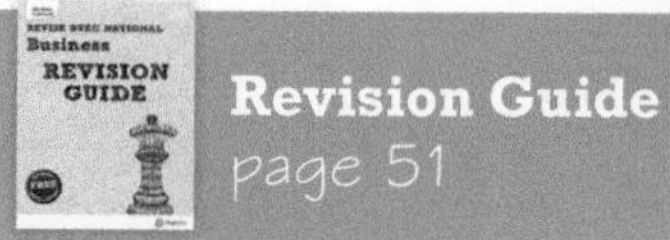

Revision Guide page 51

Hint

This question is based on the information on the previous page. Evaluate each provider and the suitability of the mortgage linked to the couple's personal and financial circumstances. Use this to support your conclusion and recommendation.

Hint

Your evaluation might use some sentences that start as follows:

The decision of which mortgage provider would be most suitable depends on the couple's personal and financial circumstances...

An analysis of each individual mortgage provider follows, matched to the couple's personal and financial circumstances...

From this analysis I conclude the couple should prioritise a mortgage provider that...

After considering all the offers from the providers, I consider the most suitable provider would be...

The reason this provider would be most suitable is because...

Revision Guide page 62

Hint

This **identify** question requires you to recall two examples. You don't need to go into detail.

Hint

Business expenditure can be divided into:

- **revenue expenditure** – the day-to-day costs of running a business
- **capital expenditure** – items bought by the business, for example vehicles, equipment.

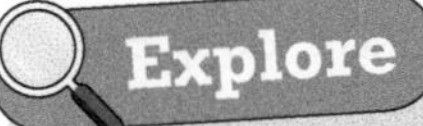

This question is asking for examples of **revenue expenditure** only.

Explore

Business expenditure results in costs which can be classified into different types:

- **fixed costs** (e.g. business rates)
- **variable costs** (e.g. raw materials)
- **semi-variable costs** (e.g. fixed telephone line rental with a variable charge based on number of calls).

SECTION B: Business Finance

Answer ALL questions.
Write your answers in the spaces provided.

7 Raj plans to start a business which prepares and delivers lunches to city centre office workers. Raj's father has offered him £2000 in cash to start the business and Raj would contribute £3000 of his own money. He has produced an outline business plan which includes both financial projections and his longer-term development plans.

Business plans such as Raj's will have a section on revenue expenditure.

Identify **two** examples of revenue expenditure Raj may have included in his outline business plan.

1 ....

....

2 ....

....

Total for Question 7 = 2 marks

8 Outline what is meant by a non-current asset.

....

....

....

....

Total for Question 8 = 2 marks

Revision Guide page 74

Hint

This **outline** question requires a brief summary of what is meant by a non-current asset. First define what a non-current asset is, then give an example or a further fact. This kind of question can usually be answered in one or two sentences.

Watch out!

An **asset** is what the business **owns** and a **liability** is what the business **owes**.

There are two types of assets: non-current and current. Current assets are for use within one year, for example cash in the safe.

Explore

You also need to know about current and non-current liabilities. A current liability is a short-term debt, e.g. a bank overdraft. A non-current liability is due after more than one year, e.g. a long-term bank loan.

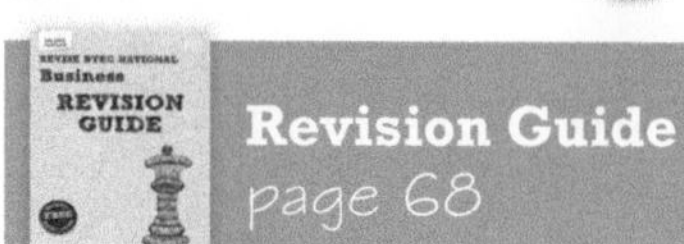

Revision Guide page 68

Hint

Calculate questions require you to work out an answer, by adding, multiplying, subtracting or dividing. It can involve the use of formulae. Here, you need to calculate figures for a cash flow forecast.

Hint

Show your workings, as marks may be given for correct workings even if your final answer is incorrect.

LEARN IT!

Cash inflow is money coming into the business, e.g. revenue from sales. Cash outflow is money going out of the business, e.g. spend on raw materials. If more money is coming in than going out, there is a net cash inflow. If more money is going out than coming in, there is a net cash outflow. A cash flow forecast therefore enables a business to identify potential cash flow problems.

9 Raj has only prepared the first four months' cash flow figures because his computer crashed and he lost some of his data. He tells you that he has a note which shows that total cash inflows in May are forecast to be £11 300 and total cash outflows are forecast to be £12 200.

(a) Calculate the missing figures in the cash flow forecast for February, March and April. These are shown by A, B and C in the table below.

3 marks

Raj's four-month cash flow forecast (£)

	Jan	**Feb**	**March**	**April**
CASH INFLOWS				
Sandwich sales	2 000	2 500	3 000	6 500
Soft drinks	500	750	1 000	1 750
Business loan			2000	
Total cash inflows	2 500	3 250	5 000	8 250
CASH OUTFLOWS				
Bread and rolls	750	900	1 120	2 400
Fillings	200	250	300	620
Soft drinks	150	225	400	700
Other operating costs	300	300	300	800
Interest payments				**(C)**
Total cash outflows	1 400	**(A)**	2 120	4 595
NET CASH INFLOW (OUTFLOW)	1 100	1 575	**(B)**	3 655
Opening balance	2 000	3 100	4 675	7 555
Closing balance	3 100	4 675	7 555	11 210

Show your workings

(b) Calculate the closing balance for May.

4 marks

Show your workings

£...

Revision Guide page 68

Hint

This question is based on the information on the previous page.

Hint

The **closing balance** in one month will be the **opening balance** in the next month. You have been given the closing balance for April in the cash flow forecast on the previous page.

Hint

Refer to the information on the previous page for the cash inflow and cash outflow figures you need to make your calculation. You need to subtract the total cash outflows from the total cash inflows for May, giving you the net cash inflow/outflow. The opening balance for May is taken from the closing balance for April. You need to take the opening balance and add the net cash inflow/outflow.

The format and order of a statement of comprehensive income is:

Sales (the revenue from the sale of goods)

Cost of sales

Gross profit = sales – cost of sales

Business expenses (operating expenses, in other words all the running costs of the business, including wages, insurance and marketing costs)

Net profit = gross profit – expenses

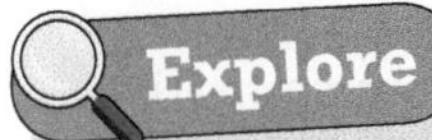

You might not always be given **the cost of sales figure**. You may need to calculate it using the following formula:

cost of sales = opening inventory + purchases – closing inventory

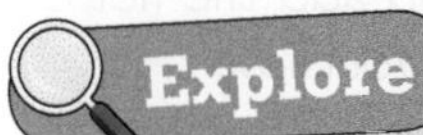

The statement of comprehensive income contains the information you need to calculate the gross profit margin and the net profit margin, as well as the mark-up. It is usually prepared each year.

Raj has given you some additional financial data and asked you to prepare the business's projected statement of comprehensive income after the first year of trading.

Projected costs and revenue after one year of trading	
Costs/revenue	**£**
Rent	12 000
Advertising	200
Sales	75 800
Insurance	422
Heating and lighting	1 250
Cost of sales	49 649
Transport	1 450
Loan interest	675
Printing	745
Office supplies	1 450

(c) Complete the projected statement of comprehensive income of the business using the following table.

8 marks

Projected statement of comprehensive income		
	£	**£**

(d) Calculate the gross profit margin, the mark-up and the net profit margin.

3 marks

Show your workings

Total for Question 9 = 18 marks

Revision Guide page 76 and 77

Hint

This question is based on the information on the previous page. The information to calculate gross profit, net profit and mark-up can be found in the **statement of comprehensive income.**

LEARN IT!

Remember the formulae for **gross and net profit:**

gross profit = sales − cost of sales

net profit = gross profit − business expenses

LEARN IT!

You won't be given any formulae in your assessment so remember them, including the **gross and net profit margins** and **mark-up**.

gross profit margin = $\frac{\text{gross profit}}{\text{sales revenue}} \times 100$

mark-up = $\frac{\text{gross profit}}{\text{cost of sales}} \times 100$

net profit margin = $\frac{\text{net profit}}{\text{sales revenue}} \times 100$

Watch out!

Profit margins and mark-up are expressed as percentage figures, so use the % notation in your answer.

Revision Guide page 78

Hint

You can tell this question relates to the **statement of financial position** because it includes items in the liquidity capital ratio formula: current assets, inventory and current liabilities. Circle these items in the question.

Hint

Note down the items and values you have circled. Separate out any liability that is a non-current liability (for example a bank loan) as this must be subtracted from the total liabilities to give the figure for current liabilities.

LEARN IT!

Use the formula for the **liquid capital ratio** to make your calculation:

$$\text{liquid capital ratio} = \frac{\text{current assets} - \text{inventory}}{\text{current liabilities}}$$

LEARN IT!

Make sure you learn formulae as they are not given in the assessment. The formula for the current ratio is below.

$$\text{capital ratio} = \frac{\text{current assets}}{\text{current liabilities}}$$

10 By the end of his first year of trading (Year 1), Raj plans to have assets of £8000. This includes £1000 of inventory and a delivery van valued at £2500, which is to be depreciated by 10% in future years using the reducing balance method. The remainder of the assets are in cash balances. The business has liabilities of £4500. This includes one non-current liability, a bank loan of £2000.

(a) Calculate the liquid capital ratio.

4 marks

Show your workings

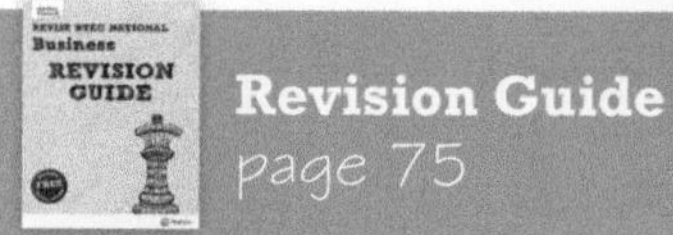

(b) Calculate the net book value of the delivery van that will be shown in the following year's statement of financial position (Year 2).

2 marks

Show your workings

£..

Total for Question 10 = 6 marks

Revision Guide page 75

Hint

This question is based on the information on the previous page, which tells you which depreciation method to use.

LEARN IT!

There are two methods for calculating depreciation.

For example, if a machine costs £25 000 with a life of five years:

Straight line depreciation allocates the amount to be depreciated using a fixed amount each year, such as £5000 for five years.

Reducing balance depreciation applies a fixed percentage rate of depreciation each year for five years (such as 20%).

Year 1: 20% of £25 000 = £5000.

Value of machine carried forward
= £25 000 − £5000
= £20 000

Year 2: 20% of £20 000 = £4000.

Value of machine carried forward
= £20 000 − £4000
= £16 000 etc

Depreciation is a **business cost**. It appears in the statement of comprehensive income as business expenses. It also appears in the statement of financial position, where it reduces the value of non-current assets.

Revision Guide
page 68

Hint

This **discuss** question requires you to consider different aspects of limitations of a cash flow forecast. You could start with the purpose of a cash flow forecast as a useful tool, then discuss the limitations. A conclusion is not required.

Hint

Think about limitations of a cash flow forecast and expand each point to say why it is a limitation or the impact of the limitation on the business. For example:

- Cash inflows may not be accurate because some customers may choose to pay on credit using a credit card.
- Costs may rise over the period of the forecast, resulting in an increase in cash outflows.

11 Raj has reviewed his cash flow forecast and considers that the figures show that the business has healthy cash balances at the end of most months.

Discuss the limitations of a cash flow forecast that Raj needs to be made aware of.

....

....

....

....

....

....

....

....

....

....

....

....

Total for Question 11 = 6 marks

12 Raj has plans to develop the business by producing and selling ready-prepared meals. He has asked you for your advice.

Analyse how a business could use break-even analysis to help them plan and develop to the next stage.

....

....

....

....

....

....

....

....

....

....

....

....

....

....

....

....

....

....

....

....

....

....

Total for Question 12 = 8 marks

Revision Guide pages 70–71

Hint

This **analyse** question requires a detailed examination. Show the links and relationship between parts of your answer.

Hint

It would be useful to refer to the break-even formula in this analysis question to show that you understand the concept of contribution. The **break-even formulae** can be calculated in units and sales revenue.

number of units sold at the break-even point

$$= \frac{\text{fixed costs}}{\text{contribution per unit}}$$

$$= \frac{\text{fixed costs}}{\text{selling price} - \text{variable cost per unit}}$$

sales revenue at break-even point = break-even units × selling price per unit

LEARN IT!

You need to be able to analyse how changes in sales and costs influence the break-even point. Business strategy could involve increasing sales and reducing costs, resulting in increased profits. Promotional activities could increase sales, whilst cheaper supplies could reduce costs.

Revision Guide pages 64–65

Hint

In this **assess** question, you could start with the different features of leasing and hire purchase as methods of purchasing non-current assets. Then weigh up short-term and long-term advantages and disadvantages, leading to your conclusion.

LEARN IT!

You need to know the difference between internal and external sources of business finance:

Internal finance is generated from the business's own finances, such as profits or selling off assets.

External finance is provided from outside the business. Leasing and hire purchase are forms of external finance.

Explore

You need to know the short-term and long-term advantages and disadvantages of other sources of external finance: loans, crowd-funding, mortgages, venture capital, debt factoring, owner's capital, trade credit, grants, donations, peer-to-peer lending, invoice discounting.

13 If Raj decides to take forward his plans to develop the business and produce ready-prepared meals, he will require specialist kitchen equipment. Raj's father has advised him to lease the equipment, but Raj considers that hire purchase would make more business sense.

Assess leasing and hire purchase methods of finance for acquiring the kitchen equipment.

....

....

....

....

....

....

....

....

....

....

....

....

....

....

....

....

....

....

....

....

....

....

....

Total for Question 13 = 10 marks

14 Raj has obtained information for a local competitor who is regarded as very efficient. Raj has provided you with his latest figures and those of the competitor, and asked you to comment on the performance of his own business.

Additional information		
	Raj's business	**Competitor's business**
Trade payable days	54 days	40 days
Trade receivable days	60 days	31 days
Inventory turnover	28 days	18 days

Evaluate the performance of Raj's business based upon the additional information he has presented.

....

....

....

....

....

....

....

....

....

....

....

....

....

....

....

....

....

....

Total for Question 14 = 12 marks

OTAL FOR SECTION B = 64 MARKS TOTAL FOR PAPER = 100 MARKS

Revision Guide page 79

Hint

When you **evaluate** business performance, you weigh up information in relation to its context, leading to a supported judgement and conclusion. Questions that require you to evaluate business performance may cover any of these three aspects: profitability, efficiency and liquidity. This question focuses on **efficiency and efficiency ratios.**

LEARN IT!

Business performance can be measured in three main ways:

Profitability: Gross profit; net profit; profit margins and Return on Capital Employed (ROCE).

Efficiency: Inventory turnover; trade payables days; trade receivables days.

Liquidity: Current ratio; liquid capital ratio.

Explore

Sometimes a business's performance may be strong in one area but weak in another. Also, a strong performance in one area could result in weak performance in another area. Trade receivables can be influenced by discounts resulting in lower profit margins.

Revision Guide page 46

Hint

This **give** question requires a factual answer with no explanations. Give the answer and move on. If unsure, check your answer at the end if you have time.

Hint

A person's approach to managing their money will depend upon a number of factors. These may relate to the economy or a person's circumstances, for example. To start you off, one factor is interest rates.

Explore

Life stages can be particularly important in later questions in Section A. People have different priorities at different times. Young people may find it difficult to save. Older people may have fewer personal debts, but may rely on a pension rather than wages.

Practice assessment 2

SECTION A: Personal Finance

Answer ALL questions.
Write your answers in the spaces provided.

1 Saving requires an individual to sacrifice some current spending to generate additional funds they can access in the future.

Give **two** factors that will influence a person's attitude towards savings.

1 ....

....

2 ....

....

Total for Question 1 = 2 marks

Revision Guide page 49

2 Describe **two** features of a store card.

1 ....

....

2 ....

....

Total for Question 2 = 2 marks

Hint

This **describe** question requires only a **brief** answer with no explanation.

Watch out!

Do not describe more than **two** features.

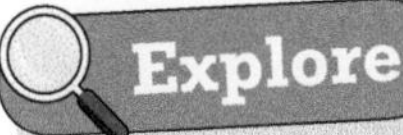

Explore

In addition to store cards, you need to know other payment methods for goods and services, and their advantages and disadvantages:

- cash
- cards (debit, credit, contactless, pre-paid, charge card)
- cheque (issued to bank customers who have a current account)
- standing orders and direct debits (instruction to pay)
- mobile banking (online app requiring access to a smart phone or tablet)
- electronic payment bank to bank (direct payment, Banker's Automated Clearing Service (BACS), Faster Payment Service (FPS), Clearing House Automated Payment System (CHAPS)).

If asked about advantages and disadvantages of each, consider for example convenience, costs, risks.

Revision Guide
page 49

Hint

This **explain** question requires you to give clear details and reasons. **First** identify the feature, **then** link the explanation. You could use 'linking words' such as 'as a result....' or 'which means...' or 'with the advantage that...'.

Hint

You could explain features associated with instant, remote access.

Explore

Be aware of some limitations to mobile banking, such as limited access to some of the services offered by a bank. Convenience and security issues may be particularly relevant when considering mobile or online banking.

Explore

Mobile banking with the use of apps offered by major banks is closely associated with online banking. Updates and additional features are often developed. You could revise online and offline payment methods offered by banks in a group, including cards, cheques and cash payments.

3 Explain **two** features of mobile banking.

1 ....

....

....

....

2 ....

....

....

....

Total for Question 3 = 4 marks

4 In 2017 home ownership in England fell to its lowest level in 30 years. The growing gap between earnings and property prices has created a housing crisis that extends beyond London to cities including Manchester.

Discuss how a building society can help a person achieve their long-term financial targets.

Total for Question 4 = 6 marks

Revision Guide page 54

Hint

When you **discuss** you consider different aspects of a topic, how they link and the extent to which they are important. A conclusion is not required.

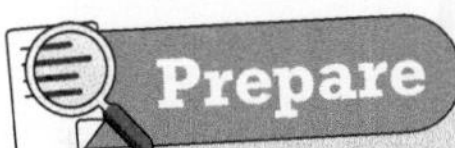

Prepare

Briefly plan a balanced answer that includes pros and cons. Here is an example:

- special features of a building society (such as specialist financial products)
- benefits to customers in achieving long-term financial targets (such as savings accounts, mortgages)
- possible limitations (such as financial products and number of branches may not be as wide as a bank).

Explore

Revise features and types of other financial organisations, and their advantages and disadvantages, such as banks, credit unions, National Savings and Investments, insurance companies, pension companies, pawnbrokers, payday loans.

Revision Guide
pages 48 and 51

Hint

This **assess** question requires careful consideration. Weigh up your points and arrive at a conclusion.

Hint

Include in your assessment the features of credit cards, such as who issues them, their use by credit holders, credit limits, interest periods/rates and paying off the balance.

Hint

Assess the **advantages** of using a credit card responsibly as part of a planned budget.

Hint

Read the information with the question, which refers to increases in outstanding debt. Assess the **disadvantages** of a credit card and difficulties in managing personal debt.

Hint

Consider the benefits of personal budgeting to **plan expenditure** and the risks of not doing so, such as debt, credit rating for a loan, generating income to save.

5 In the UK in June 2017 outstanding credit card debt stood at £68.5bn, up by £900m from the end of March.

Assess the use of credit cards in personal budgeting.

....

....

....

....

....

....

....

....

....

....

....

....

....

....

....

....

....

....

....

....

....

....

....

....

....

....

Total for Question 5 = 10 marks

6 Mr and Mrs Foster have recently booked their annual two-week holiday in Spain. The total cost of their holiday is £5000. Mr Foster prefers to use his credit card on holiday, keeping £200 in foreign currency for emergency use. This is divided equally between himself and his wife. Loss of the credit card is covered by the credit-card company. Mrs Foster is recovering from recent knee surgery following an injury playing football. They are now looking to purchase a suitable travel insurance policy. They have used a price-comparison site to obtain information on the insurance cover provided, including the policy excesses. These excesses are the amount of any insured loss that would have to be met using the Fosters' personal finances.

This table gives information on travel insurance policies being considered by the Fosters.

Summary of travel insurance terms and conditions			
Provider	**Features**	**Policy excesses**	**Basic cost**
ProAchieve Insurers	Cancellation: up to £4 000	£200	£300
	Holiday interruption: £1 500	£100	
	Baggage delay: £15 per day	£40	
	Travel delay: £5 per day	Nil	
	Hospital daily benefit: £45	Nil	
	Personal money: £1 000	£200	
	Multi-trip insurance		
Shales Insurance Services	Cancellation: £5 000	£400	£425
	Holiday interruption: £1 000	£50	
	Baggage delay: £20 per day	£20	
	Travel delay: £30 per day	Nil	
	Hospital daily benefit: £50	Nil	
	Personal money: £2 000	£100	
	Worldwide cover		
Laminster Insurance Ltd	Cancellation: £3 000	£50	£325
	Holiday interruption: £2 500	£100	
	Baggage delay: £10 per day	£20	
	Travel delay: £10 per day	Nil	
	Hospital daily benefit: £100	Nil	
	Personal money: £400	£100	
Expeditions Insurance Ltd	Cancellation: £5 250	£150	£375
	Holiday interruption: £2 000	£200	
	Baggage delay: £8 per day	£16	
	Travel delay: £20 per day	Nil	
	Hospital daily benefit: £50	Nil	
	Personal money: £500	£50	

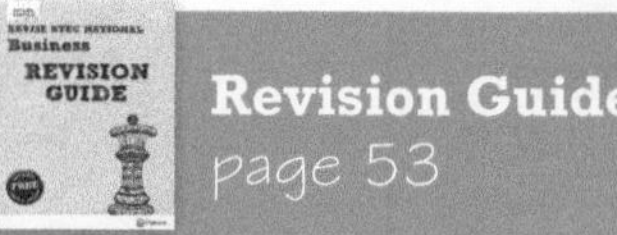

Revision Guide
page 53

Hint

Read the **evaluate** question on the next page. You need to evaluate information about the Fosters and information about different travel insurance policies, and come to a judgement about which is suitable.

Hint

Insurance relates to the risks of certain events occurring. Evaluate the risks faced by the Fosters in relation to their holiday arrangements. Circle **personal circumstances**. Underline **financial circumstances**. Decide how each one may influence their choice.

Hint

Evaluate the **relevance** of each policy to the Fosters. Note as unsuitable any insurance cover not relevant. Evaluate those remaining to determine which provides best value for money for suitable cover for their needs.

Watch out!

The lowest premium (the cost of insurance) may not always provide the best value for money.

Revision Guide page 53

Hint

This question is based on the information on the previous page. Evaluate each policy and the suitability of the travel insurance linked to the Fosters' personal and financial circumstances. Use this to support your conclusion and recommendation.

Watch out!

Not all risks covered by the policies may be relevant for the Foster family.

Hint

Your evaluation might use some sentences that start as follows:

The decision of which travel insurance would be most suitable depends on the Fosters' personal and financial circumstances...

An analysis of each type of travel insurance follows, matched to the Fosters' personal and financial circumstances...

From this analysis I conclude the Fosters should prioritise an insurance policy that...

After considering all the policies, I consider the most suitable provider would be...

The reason this travel insurance policy would be most suitable is because...

Evaluate which travel insurance would be most suitable for the Fosters.

....

....

....

....

....

....

....

....

....

....

....

....

....

....

....

....

....

....

....

....

....

....

....

....

....

....

Total for Question 6 = 12 marks

TOTAL FOR SECTION A = 36 MARKS

SECTION B: Business Finance

Answer ALL questions.
Write your answers in the spaces provided.

7 Bilal started up his own bicycle repair and sales shop, *Bilal's Bikes*, last year. His business is located in a rented workshop in the town centre. It provides a bicycle repair service for office workers who cycle into work. In addition, he sells a range of spare parts and cycling clothing.

Bilal is now in the process of drawing together his financial records to determine the performance of his business after its first year of trading.

Identify **two** current assets Bilal may have included in his financial records.

1 ....

....

2 ....

....

Total for Question 7 = 2 marks

Revision Guide page 74

Hint

This **identify** question requires you to recall what current assets are, and to identify two examples. You don't need to go into detail.

Hint

Read the information about the business. Here you are given the business name, who owns it, what it does, where it is located and how long it has existed. Further questions build on the opening information, so make sure you understand it.

LEARN IT!

Assets are what a business owns. They are divided into current assets and non-current assets. Current assets are for use within one year. Non-current assets are ones you expect to own for more than one year (such as machinery).

Explore

The value of a business's assets appears in its statement of financial position. Non-current assets are subject to depreciation.

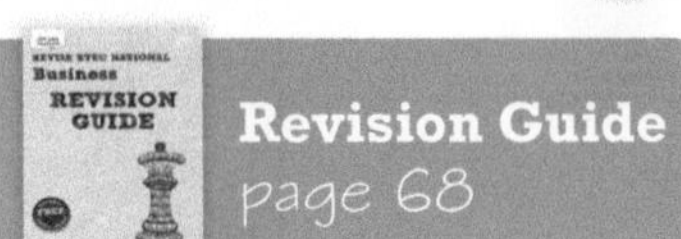

Revision Guide page 68

Hint

Your answer to this question should **outline** the benefits of what the cash flow forecast shows Bilal and how it helps him as the business owner.

Hint

You are not required to produce a cash flow forecast, but should use appropriate financial terms, such as cash inflows and cash outflows.

LEARN IT!

Cash flow forecasts are used to predict the cash inflows and outflows for a business over a period of time. In any month, a **net cash inflow** arises when the business forecasts it will receive more cash than it has spent, whereas a **net cash outflow** arises when it forecasts it will spend more cash than it predicts to receive.

8 Outline the benefits to Bilal's business of producing a cash flow forecast.

....

....

....

....

Total for Question 8 = 2 marks

9 Bilal has provided the following information regarding the business.

(a) Calculate

(i) total assets

(ii) current ratio

(iii) liquid capital ratio.

3 marks

Bilal's business	
Non-current assets	£7 250
Current assets	£8 000
Inventory	£2 000
Current liabilities	£2 000
Non-current liabilities	£3 000

Show your workings

Hint

Calculate questions require you to work out an answer, by adding, multiplying, subtracting or dividing. It can involve use of formulae. Marks may be given for correct workings even if your final answer is incorrect.

LEARN IT!

The total value of what a business owns (total assets) can be calculated by the following formula:

total assets = current assets + non-current assets

Remember that inventory is **included** in the figure for current assets.

Use the correct formulae for the **current ratio** and the **liquid capital ratio**:

$$\text{current ratio} = \frac{\text{current assets}}{\text{current liabilities}}$$

$$\text{liquid capital ratio} = \frac{\text{current assets} - \text{inventory}}{\text{current liabilities}}$$

Explore

Know the difference between the current ratio and the liquid capital ratio. The liquid capital ratio doesn't include inventory, so is a more accurate measure of a business's ability to pay its short-term debts.

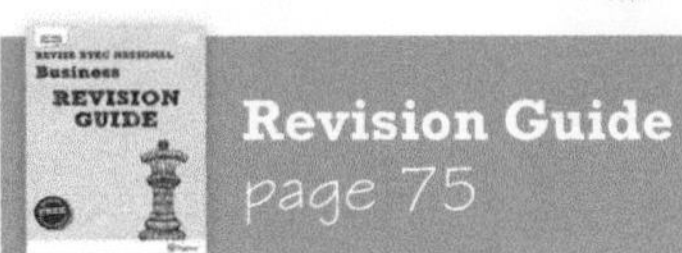

Revision Guide page 75

LEARN IT!

There are two methods for calculating depreciation.

For example, if a machine costs £25 000, with a life of five years:

Straight line depreciation allocates the amount to be depreciated using a fixed amount each year, e.g. £5000 for five years. Where an asset has a residual value, **the annual depreciation** is calculated using the formula:

$$\frac{\text{asset purchase price} - \text{estimated salvage value}}{\text{estimated useful life of the asset}}$$

Reducing balance depreciation applies a fixed percentage rate of depreciation each year for five years (e.g. 20%).

Year 1: 20% of £25 000 = £5000.

Value of machine carried forward = £25 000 − £5000 = £20 000

Year 2: 20% of £20 000 = £4000.

Value of machine carried forward = £20 000 − £4000 = £16 000 etc.

Explore

The annual depreciation amount for both methods will be shown in the statement of comprehensive income as an expense.

During the year, Bilal purchased a delivery van which he uses to collect spare parts from his suppliers. The van was bought for £4000 with a useful life of four years and an estimated salvage value of £500.

(b) Calculate the net book value of the delivery van in each year of its useful life using the straight-line depreciation method.

4 marks

Show your workings

Bilal has lost some of his financial records, but he remembers that he worked out his gross profit margin as 20%. His incomplete records are as follows. The missing information is shown by A, B, C, D.

Extract from statement of comprehensive income		
Sales		£96 000
Less cost of sales		
Opening inventory	£19 500	
Add purchases	£68 700	
	£88 200	
Less closing inventory	**(C)**	
		(B)
Gross profit		**(A)**
Expenses	**(D)**	
Net profit		**£12 900**

(c) Complete the extract from the statement of comprehensive income by calculating the missing values for A, B, C and D.

8 marks

Show your workings

Revision Guide page 72

Hint

A The gross profit can be calculated using the figure for the gross profit margin (20%).

B This is the total cost of sales. When the gross profit figure is known, find the difference between the sales figure and the gross profit figure.

C Once the cost of sales is known (B), the closing inventory can be calculated using the formula:

Cost of sales (B) = opening inventory (given) + purchases (given) − closing inventory (C)

D Calculate the difference between the gross profit and the net profit to establish how much the business has spent on expenses.

LEARN IT!

Use these formulae for **profit margins** to answer the question:

gross profit margin = $\frac{\text{gross profit}}{\text{sales revenue}} \times 100$

net profit = gross profit − expenses

Revision Guide page 79

Hint

This question is based on the information on the previous page. You need to use your answers to Question 9(c) to complete the calculation.

Hint

Make sure you show your workings by starting off with the formula for inventory turnover. Even if you haven't calculated the figures correctly in Question 9(c) you may be awarded marks for stating the formula.

LEARN IT!

You need to know the formula for the **inventory turnover**:

$$\frac{\text{average inventory}}{\text{cost of sales}} \times 365$$

Hint

You can calculate the **average inventory** by adding together the value of the opening inventory and the value of the closing inventory then dividing by 2 as follows:

$$\text{average inventory} = \frac{\text{opening inventory} + \text{closing inventory}}{2}$$

(d) Calculate the inventory turnover (in days) for the business.

3 marks

Show your workings

Total for Question 9 = 18 marks

10 Bilal has designed a lightweight saddle which he wants to start to assemble using component parts. He proposes to sell the saddles for £20 and he estimates sales to be 1152 units per year with output spread evenly over the course of the year. His fixed costs will be £2000 and his variable costs will be £12 per unit.

(a) Calculate how many saddles Bilal will need to sell in order to break even.

4 marks

Show your workings

Revision Guide
page 70

Hint

Use the formula for the **break-even point** in this question:

break-even point = $\frac{\text{fixed costs}}{\text{contribution per unit}}$

Hint

The contribution per unit can be calculated by the following formulae:

contribution per unit = selling price per unit − variable cost per unit

Explore

You need to be able to explain how the break-even point is affected by changes in costs, sales and price, and how the business can adjust its strategy to reduce costs and increase sales.

Explore

You need to know what is meant by the margin of safety, which is the difference between the actual level of sales and the break-even point. The margin of safety provides a buffer against making a loss.

Revision Guide
page 70

Hint

This question is based on the information on the previous page.

LEARN IT!

Use the following formula for **the number of months to break even** to answer this question:

$$\text{months of break even} = \frac{\text{break-even units}}{\text{units produced per month}}$$

Explore

You need to show how break-even analysis can be used by a business to plan, monitor and control its activities. It is a useful planning tool for setting targets relating to costs, sales and profits.

Explore

You need to know how to perform other calculations using financial data relating to **break-even analysis**:

margin of safety = planned or actual sales − break-even point

total contribution = contribution per unit × number of units sold

total revenue = quantity of goods sold × selling price per unit

At the break-even point:
total revenue = total costs

(b) Calculate the number of months before the new product will break even.

2 marks

Show your workings

Total for Question 10 = 6 marks

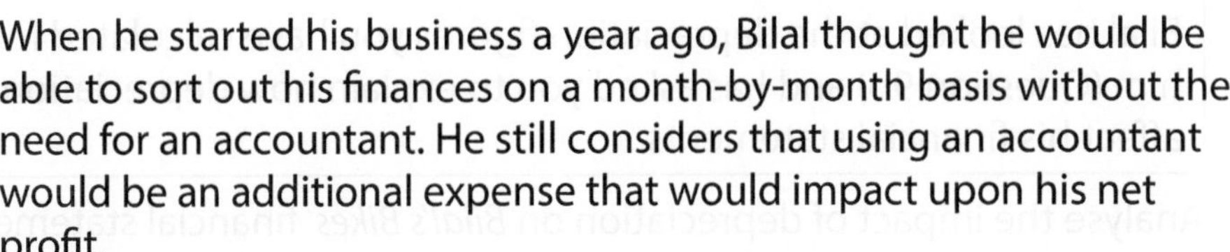

11 When he started his business a year ago, Bilal thought he would be able to sort out his finances on a month-by-month basis without the need for an accountant. He still considers that using an accountant would be an additional expense that would impact upon his net profit.

Discuss the reasons Bilal might consider for employing the services of an accountant.

....

....

....

....

....

....

....

....

....

....

....

....

Total for Question 11 = 6 marks

Revision Guide page 59

Hint

This **discuss** question requires a well-developed, balanced and logical discussion of reasons for using an accountant, weighing up value for money against fees that add to expenses.

Hint

Include your understanding of how an additional expense impacts on net profit. Use financial terminology such as 'cash flow forecasts', 'trade receivables', and 'trade payables', and reference the main financial documents.

Explore

You need to know the services provided by an accountant and how they contribute to the efficient operation of a business:

- recording transactions
- management of business (planning, monitoring, controlling)
- compliance (preventing fraud, compliance with law)
- measuring performance
- control (trade receivables, trade payables, preventing fraud).

Revision Guide pages 72-75

Hint

When you **analyse** you give a detailed examination and breakdown of a topic. Show you are aware of how depreciation is accounted for (straight line and reducing balance).

Hint

You need to consider the **impact of depreciation** on the two main financial statements: the statement of comprehensive income and the statement of financial position. Your analysis should show that you understand how depreciation is recorded in each financial statement.

Hint

Use **financial terminology** in your answer, such as 'expenses', 'non-current assets', 'net profit' and 'net book value'.

Explore

Make sure you know the information contained in the two main financial statements and how to prepare each of the statements from a set of given data.

12 Bilal has looked at the depreciation figures you have calculated for him (Question 9b) and has asked you to explain how depreciation will affect his financial statements.

Analyse the impact of depreciation on *Bilal's Bikes'* financial statements.

....

....

....

....

....

....

....

....

....

....

....

....

....

....

....

....

Total for Question 12 = 8 marks

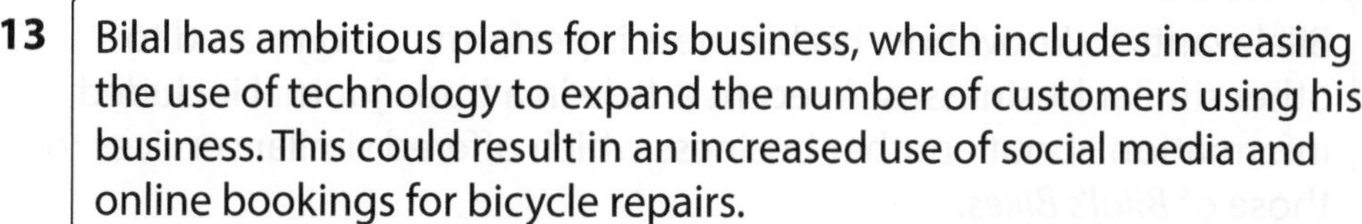

13 Bilal has ambitious plans for his business, which includes increasing the use of technology to expand the number of customers using his business. This could result in an increased use of social media and online bookings for bicycle repairs.

Assess the different sources of internal and external finance that Bilal could consider to support his future plans for the business.

....

....

....

....

....

....

....

....

....

....

....

....

....

....

....

....

....

....

....

....

....

....

....

Total for Question 13 = 10 marks

Revision Guide pages 63-65

Hint

Your answer to this **assess** question should show you know what sources of internal and external finance are, and which one is best to use. Then assess the available sources of finance. Weigh up how different sources of finance may be more suited to the different types of expenditure. Consider the short and longer term. Arrive at a conclusion.

Hint

Business finance is available from external creditors (those providing finance) as well as the business's own financial resources.

Explore

You need to know internal sources of business finance (such as retained profits, reserves, selling off assets) and external sources (such as bank loans, overdrafts, trade credit, leasing, hire purchase). Know their features, short-term and long-term advantages and disadvantages, and which source of finance is most appropriate for different situations.

Revision Guide pages 76–79

Hint

This **evaluate** question is asking you to consider evidence of performance of Bilal's business against a similar business and draw a conclusion.

Hint

These performance indicators cover three main areas: profits (ROCE), efficiency (trade receivables and trade payables days) and liquidity (current ratio). Look at each ratio in turn and comment on the performance of both businesses to identify good features.

Hint

Evaluate the reasons why Bilal's business might be doing better or worse than *Wally's Wheels* and the implications for profit, efficiency and liquidity.

Explore

You need to know how the different measures of performance relating to profitability, efficiency and liquidity can impact upon a business and the measures that the business can take to improve each of the performance measures.

14 Bilal wants to know how his business is performing compared to other similar businesses. A recent article in a trade journal included information about another business which offered similar services to those of *Bilal's Bikes*.

Additional information		
	Bilal's Bikes	**Wally's Wheels**
Current ratio	1.75:1	1.53:1
Mark-up	25%	30%
ROCE	5%	7%
Trade payable days	32 days	30 days
Trade receivable days	42 days	37 days

Evaluate the performance of *Bilal's Bikes* compared to *Wally's Wheels* based upon the additional information he has presented.

....

....

....

....

....

....

....

....

....

....

....

....

....

....

....

....

....

Total for Question 14 = 12 marks

TOTAL FOR SECTION B = 64 MARKS TOTAL FOR PAPER = 100 MARKS

Practice assessment 3

SECTION A: Personal Finance

Answer ALL questions.
Write your answers in the spaces provided.

1 An individual's priorities will change as they go through different stages in their life.

Give **two** reasons why a person should plan their personal finances.

1 ....

....

2 ....

....

Total for Question 1 = 2 marks

Revision Guide
page 47

Hint

This **give** question requires you to recall two reasons. You do not need to go into detail. One reason could be based on the benefit of planning and one reason could be based on the risk of not planning.

Hint

Consider the advantages of savings, and the consequences of overspending and getting into debt.

Explore

Planning personal finances and budgets involves mapping expenditure priorities against income so money is allocated to the most important items. The role of money and a person's view of budgeting may change over their life history. Factors that can influence a person's attitudes include culture, life stages, life events, interest rates and external influences.

Revision Guide page 50

Hint

This **describe** question only needs a brief answer. No explanation is required. Do not describe more than two features.

Hint

A packaged bank account contains additional features not available with an ordinary current account. Account holders pay a fee to cover the additional features.

Explore

You also need to know the features, advantages and disadvantages, and different services offered for other types of current account:

- standard current account (e.g. features for customers with a fair credit rating)
- student account (e.g. features aimed at learners in higher education)
- basic account (e.g. limited features for customers with a poor credit rating).

2 Describe **two** features of a packaged current account.

1 ....

....

2 ....

....

Total for Question 2 = 2 marks

3 Explain **two** functions of the Financial Conduct Authority (FCA).

1 ....

....

....

....

2 ....

....

....

....

Total for Question 3 = 4 marks

Revision Guide page 57

Hint

This **explain** question requires a clear answer with some linked detail. **First** identify a function of the FCA, **then** link the explanation.

Hint

Until April 2014, the Office of Fair Trading was responsible for protecting consumer interests. This part of its work is now the responsibility of the FCA.

Explore

Revise legislation surrounding consumer protection. One example is the Consumer Credit Act (1974) that regulates credit card purchases and provides consumer protection.

Revision Guide
page 52

Hint

This **discuss** question requires you to consider different aspects of investing in shares, how they interrelate and the extent to which they are important.

Prepare

An answer plan can be helpful. For example:

- benefits of shares (e.g. payment of dividends)
- drawbacks of shares (e.g. impact of the loss of value in the shares).

4 Shareholders are one of the main stakeholders in the business community, taking risks in exchange for financial returns.

Discuss the factors that an investor should consider when purchasing shares.

....

....

....

....

....

....

....

....

....

....

....

....

Total for Question 4 = 6 marks

5 The proportion of bank customers using the internet to deal with their bank has grown significantly over the last few years, whilst the number of high street banks has declined.

Assess the advantages and disadvantages of online banking.

....

....

....

....

....

....

....

....

....

....

....

....

....

....

....

....

....

....

....

....

....

....

....

....

Total for Question 5 = 10 marks

Revision Guide page 56

Hint

When you **assess** you present a careful consideration of different factors. Here, you need to weigh up the advantages and disadvantages of online banking as a method of interacting with customers, and come to a conclusion.

Hint

Start with the features of online banking and how it is used. When you assess the advantages and disadvantages, consider aspects such as access, security and limitations.

Explore

Revise other ways that customers can interact with their banks:

- bank branches (e.g. full range of face-to-face services)
- telephone banking (e.g. simple transactions, often automated)
- postal banking (e.g. statements, cheques)
- mobile banking (e.g. using an app).

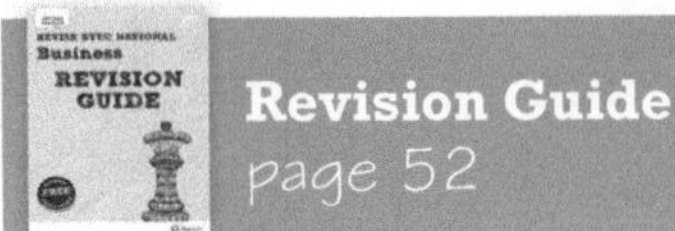

Revision Guide page 52

Hint

Read the **evaluate** question on the next page. You need to evaluate information about the needs of Ling and Mark and information about the different savings products, and come to a judgement about which is suitable.

Hint

Make sure you understand Ling and Mark's situation. Circle the **personal circumstances**. Underline the **financial circumstances**. Decide how each one will influence their choice of savings product (for example how much they need to save for their wedding; when they need to access savings).

Watch out!

Look for any special conditions on high interest savings accounts.

Hint

Ling and Mark can switch savings between accounts if they can get a better rate – but consider the access they may need to their money.

6 Ling and Mark have announced their engagement and plan to get married in two years' time. Ling's parents have recently won a large sum of money on Premium Bonds, their first win in five years, and have given the couple £10 000 towards the cost of their wedding. Interest rates are forecast to increase over the next year and the couple have begun to research suitable ways to invest the money. Given Ling's parents' recent good fortune, one method of saving they are considering is the purchase of Premium Bonds.

They have to take into account that the hotel where the wedding reception will be held requires a deposit of £1800 payable six months before the wedding. They also need to budget for a photographer and entertainers, who will also need to be paid before the wedding takes place, sometimes up to a year in advance. They have set aside £1500 for these additional costs.

They have estimated the total cost of their wedding as £20 000.

This table records the information collected by Ling and Mark.

Summary of savings products, and terms and conditions			
Provider	**Product**	**Interest rate**	**Features**
Exmouth Building Society	One year fixed rate ISA	1.6%	After a year the rate reduces to the standard variable rate, currently 0.75%
Clynedale Bank	Instant access account	1.7%	Includes a bonus of 0.8% for the first six months after which the rate reduces to the standard variable rate, currently 0.7%
Ferris Bank	Instant access account	1.25%	3% cashback on purchases when using the bank's credit card
NS&I	Premium Bonds	Variable – dependent on number of wins	Tax-free monthly cash prizes up to £1 million

Evaluate which savings methods would be most suitable for Ling and Mark.

Total for Question 6 = 12 marks

TOTAL FOR SECTION A = 36 MARKS

Revision Guide page 52

Hint

This question is based on the information on the previous page. Evaluate each product and the suitability of the savings methods linked to the couple's personal and financial circumstances. Use this to support your conclusion(s) and recommendation(s).

Watch out!

There may not be one correct answer, so cover advantages and disadvantages of your chosen option(s).

Hint

Your evaluation might use some sentences that start as follows:

The decision of which savings methods would be most suitable depends on the couple's personal and financial circumstances...

They should consider the following factors for where to deposit their savings...

They should not focus only on the highest interest rates because...

An analysis of each savings product follows, matched to the couple's personal and financial circumstances...

After considering all the products, I consider the most suitable would be...

The reason the savings product(s) would be most suitable is because...

Revision Guide page 60

Hint

Read the opening information with details about a business. Here you are given the business name, who owns it, what it does and future plans. Further questions build on the opening information, so make sure you understand it.

Hint

This **identify** question requires you to recall what revenue income is and give two examples. You don't need to go into detail.

Watch out!

You need to know the difference between revenue income and capital income.

Revenue income is received by the business on sales of its goods or services.

Capital income includes loans, mortgages, shares, owner's capital and debentures. Capital income is a long-term investment.

SECTION B: Business Finance

Answer ALL questions.
Write your answers in the spaces provided.

7 Vanessa started her fitness business, *Keep in Shape*, after leaving college. The business has a loyal customer base, including a number of corporate clients. Vanessa employs three part-time personal trainers and last year began selling sports clothing sourced from a low-cost supplier of designer clothes in China, who provides trade credit of 20 days on each order. Vanessa has plans to move into larger premises, which would enable her to expand her sales of sports clothing. Last financial year the business made a net profit of £5880.

Financing the move into larger premises will require Vanessa to secure additional external finance and she has asked you to comment on her future plans for the business.

Identify **two** types of revenue income.

1 ....

....

2 ....

....

Total for Question 7 = 2 marks

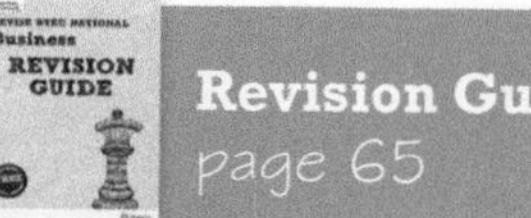

8 Outline one benefit of trade credit for a small business.

....

....

....

....

Total for Question 8 = 2 marks

Revision Guide page 65

Hint

This **outline** question requires a brief overview. You don't need to go into detail.

Hint

Trade credit is a form of business finance. It is similar to the concept of 'buy now pay later', but usually only between businesses.

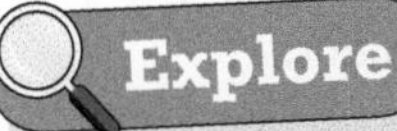

Explore

In the statement of financial position, trade credit will appear either as:

- a trade receivable, if the business has given trade credit to a customer
- a trade payable, if the business has received trade credit from a supplier.

Explore

The amount of days given for payment can vary. A business might aim to collect payments from customers in fewer days than they pay suppliers. They may also change the payment terms if they have to pay their suppliers more quickly than they collect money from customers.

Revision Guide pages 76 and 77

Hint

Calculate questions require you to work out an answer, by adding, multiplying, subtracting or dividing. This can involve the use of formulae.

LEARN IT!

You need to learn the formulae for the **gross profit margin** and **net profit margin** because they will not be given to you in the assessment.

$$\text{gross profit margin} = \frac{\text{gross profit}}{\text{sales revenue}} \times 100$$

$$\text{net profit margin} = \frac{\text{net profit}}{\text{sales revenue}} \times 100$$

Watch out!

Gross and net profit margins are usually calculated as percentages. Make sure that you show your workings.

Explore

Gross profit and net profit are included in the statement of financial income, so you can calculate profit margins by extracting information from this financial statement.

9 Vanessa's bank manager has asked her to provide information on the forecast profitability of increasing the sales of sports clothing, including the gross profit margin and the net profit margin. She has provided you with the following forecasts and asked you to help her work out the figures.

(a) Calculate the gross profit margin and the net profit margin.

3 marks

Additional information	
Sales	£42 000
Cost of sales	£16 800
Insurance	£1 250
Advertising	£870
Rent	£7 200
Wages	£10 000

Show your workings

The bank manager has suggested that changes in the exchange rate of the pound will increase the cost of imported goods over the next year, resulting in an increase in Vanessa's cost of sales.

(b) Calculate the mark-up on the sports clothes if the forecast cost of sales increases by 5%.

4 marks

Show your workings

Revision Guide page 76

Hint

The forecast cost of sales is shown in the table on the previous page as £16 800, so you need to increase this figure by 5%.

LEARN IT!

When a business sells goods to customers, it must charge a price higher than the cost of goods in order to earn a profit. The **mark-up** of costs is the percentage of an item's wholesale cost that the retailer includes in the retail cost to make a profit.

$$\text{mark-up} = \frac{\text{gross profit}}{\text{cost of sales}} \times 100$$

The mark-up figure will be shown as a % figure.

Hint

To calculate the mark-up you will need to calculate revised figures for both cost of sales and gross profit. The 5% increase will change both these figures.

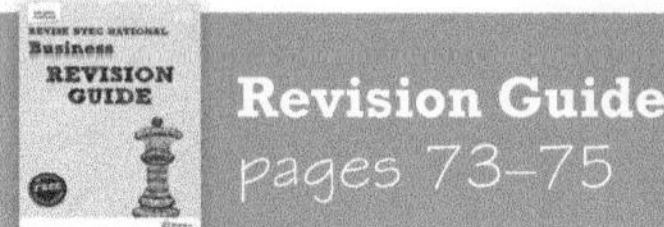
Revision Guide pages 73–75

Hint

To prepare a statement of financial position you need to have information relating to a business's assets, liabilities and capital (owner's capital plus net profit for the year). The table does not include the figure for the net profit, which is in the information with Question 9 on page 48.

Explore

Make sure you can define the categories of profit:

- gross profit: net sales minus cost of goods sold
- net profit: operating profit minus any other expenses before tax
- net profit after tax: the final profit figure once the business has met its tax liabilities
- retained profit: some of the profits kept in the business after the owner's drawings have been deducted. Drawings are funds that could be either salary or wages taken by the owner.

Explore

The **net assets** of a business can be calculated using the following formula:

net assets =
total assets (current assets + non-current liabilities) −
total liabilities (current liabilities + non-current liabilities)

In other words:

net assets =
total assets − total liabilities

Vanessa has provided you with the following financial information for the last financial year.

Additional information	
Gym equipment	£2 400
Motor vehicle	£1 200
Inventory	£1 400
Trade receivables	£1 350
Cash in bank account	£650
Owner's capital	£720
Trade payables owed to the Chinese supplier	£400

(c) Prepare Vanessa's statement of financial position for the last financial year. The net profit for the year can be found in the information given with Question 9 on page 48.

8 marks

Statement of financial position		
	£	£

You discover that Vanessa has not accounted for depreciation in last year's financial figures.

(d) Calculate the revised net profit for the year if the business's non-current assets were depreciated by 10%.

3 marks

Show your workings

£...

Total for Question 9 = 18 marks

Revision Guide pages 72, 74, 75

Hint

This question is based on the information on the previous page.

Watch out!

Don't reduce the profit figure by 10%. Depreciation will affect the net book value (NBV) of the business's non-current assets – in this case the gym equipment (£2400) and the motor vehicle (£1200).

LEARN IT!

Depreciation is a business cost and is therefore included in the statement of comprehensive income. As it will impact upon the value of a non-current asset it also has to be accounted for in the statement of financial position. The overall impact of depreciation will be to reduce the level of net profit for the year.

Explore

Depreciation can be calculated by either the straight-line method or the reducing balance method. The reducing balance method reduces the value of non-current assets by a set percentage figure each year.

Revision Guide Pages 69–70

Hint

This question requires you to use the **break-even formula** to calculate different values for fixed costs, variable costs and the selling price.

break-even in units = $\frac{\text{fixed costs}}{\text{contribution per unit}}$

Show your workings as marks may be given for correct workings even if the final answer is incorrect.

Hint

contribution per unit = selling price per unit − variable cost per unit

LEARN IT!

total contribution = contribution per unit × number of units sold

Explore

Know the benefits of using break-even analysis in planning and monitoring, and control and target-setting. For example, the business can use a break-even analysis to help work out how many units it needs to sell before it starts to make a profit. It can also be used to look at the impact of increasing or decreasing fixed or variable costs on the break-even point.

10 Vanessa is considering selling healthy meal deals in the gym as part of her expansion plans. Her variable cost per snack is £2 and her selling price is £5. She has calculated that she will need to sell 1250 meal deals to break even.

(a) Calculate Vanessa's fixed costs.

4 marks

Show your workings

£.......................................

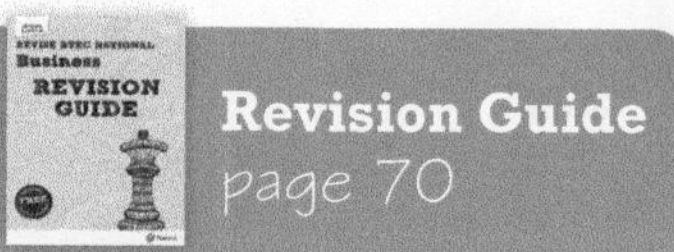

(b) Calculate the additional number of sales required above the break-even point if there was a margin of safety of 22%.

2 marks

Show your workings

Revision Guide page 70

Hint

This question is based on information given with Question 10a on the previous page, where the break-even point is given as 1250 units.

LEARN IT!

The margin of safety is calculated using the following formula:

margin of safety = sales − break-even level of output

Hint

You will need to find 22% of the break-even units.

Total for Question 10 = 6 marks

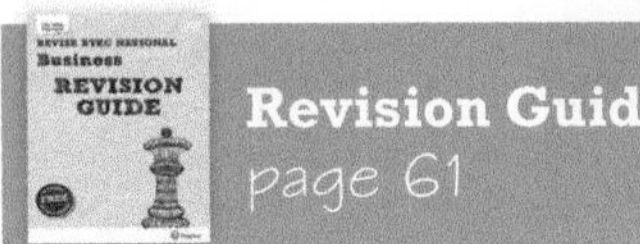

Revision Guide page 61

Hint

This **discuss** question requires you to consider the impact of different aspects of intangible assets on the value of a business. Consider how they interrelate and the extent to which they are important.

Hint

You could start by discussing the features of assets and intangible assets, then how a business benefits from them. Discuss some examples and link their influence on the value of a business to competitive advantage over business rivals.

LEARN IT!

Examples of **tangible** (physical) assets: current assets such as cash and non-current assets such as machinery.

Examples of **intangible** assets: trade secrets, patents. Intangible assets may not always be included on the statement of financial position, but they are taken into account if the business is sold.

11 When Vanessa met with her bank manager he asked her if the value of her business included any intangible assets. She was unsure how to respond and has asked for your advice.

Discuss how intangible assets can influence the value of a business.

....

....

....

....

....

....

....

....

....

....

....

....

Total for Question 11 = 6 marks

12 Moving to new business premises will result in additional costs and Vanessa is keen to understand how different types of costs will impact upon her business.

Analyse how fixed, variable and semi-variable costs can impact upon Vanessa's business decisions.

....

....

....

....

....

....

....

....

....

....

....

....

....

....

....

....

....

....

....

....

....

....

....

....

Total for Question 12 = 8 marks

Revision Guide pages 69–71

Hint

This **analysis** question requires a detailed and balanced examination. Show the relationship between fixed, variable and semi-variable costs and their impact on business decisions.

Hint

As part of your answer, consider costs on the basis of business decisions. These decisions include output, sales and price, which form part of break-even analysis.

Explore

A set of data relating to fixed and variable costs can be used to prepare a break-even chart, which can be used to show how changes in fixed or variable costs can affect the break-even point. Businesses will need to change the way they work day-to-day if the costs are changing.

Revision Guide pages 62 and 64

Hint

This **assess** question requires careful consideration of advantages and disadvantages to arrive at a conclusion.

Hint

You could consider factors in relation to whether the business is new or established.

Hint

Mortgage interest payments appear on the statement of comprehensive income as an expense, with the outstanding mortgage appearing on the statement of financial position as a non-current liability.

Hint

Consider the responsibilities for the business owner of owning business property or renting business property, and any opportunities or limitations that could arise.

Explore

Mortgages are an external source of business finance. Revise the short-term and long-term advantages and disadvantages of other external sources: owner's capital, hire purchase, debt factoring, loans, crowd-funding, venture capital, leasing, trade credit, grants, donations, peer-to-peer lending, invoice discounting.

13 One of the important business decisions which Vanessa has to make is how to finance the move into the new business premises. She has to decide between renting or purchasing new premises.

Assess the advantages and disadvantages of renting, or of purchasing new business premises with a mortgage.

....

....

....

....

....

....

....

....

....

....

....

....

....

....

....

....

....

....

....

....

....

....

Total for Question 13 = 10 marks

Revision Guide pages 77–80

14 Each year Vanessa compares her business's performance with the previous year, so she can judge how well her business has performed. The figures for the current and previous year are shown in the table below.

Additional information		
	Current year	**Previous year**
Liquid capital ratio	1.95:1	1.05:1
Trade receivable days	32	27
Inventory turnover	15	21
ROCE	8%	6%

Evaluate the performance of *Keep in Shape* based upon the four financial ratios.

Hint

For this **evaluate** question, consider evidence of performance for the current year against the previous year based on the four financial ratios and draw a conclusion.

Hint

The purpose of evaluating financial ratios is to determine whether the business is performing better or worse over time. Take each financial ratio and indicate whether, for the current year, it is a + (better performance) or a − (worse performance) when compared with the previous year.

Hint

Consider what each financial ratio is measuring and its impact on the business in terms of profit (revenue minus total cost), liquidity (ability to meet current liabilities) and efficiency (how well the business is managing its resources and systems). This will enable you to draw a conclusion in relation to each financial ratio.

Total for Question 14 = 12 marks

TOTAL FOR SECTION B = 64 MARKS TOTAL FOR PAPER = 100 MARKS

Revision Guide page 46

Time it!

Time yourself completing this practice assessment. Try to complete it within two hours. Spend around 40–45 minutes on Section A. If there is time, check your answers at the end. Details of the actual assessment may change, so check the latest guidance on the Pearson website to be sure you are up to date.

Time it!

Use the number of marks as a guide to how much time to spend on each question.

Hint

For this **give** question, recall two external factors, then move on. Explanations are not required.

Hint

External factors are beyond the control of the individual, for example the state of the economy or government policies. The value of savings includes their 'real value', which will be dependent upon the general level of prices in the economy.

Practice assessment 4

SECTION A: Personal Finance

Answer ALL questions.
Write your answers in the spaces provided.

1 People's finances can be affected by external factors which they are not able to influence or control.

Give **two** external factors that could influence the value of a person's savings.

1 ....

....

2 ....

....

Total for Question 1 = 2 marks

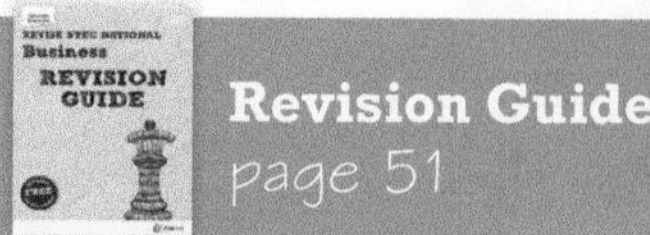

Describe **one** feature of hire purchase.

....

....

....

....

Total for Question 2 = 2 marks

Hint

For this **describe** question, answer with a main point, then develop the point. For example: used to purchase non-current assets such as machinery, where the business owner pays a deposit and interest is charged on the balance remaining. Describe another main point of hire purchase, then develop the point.

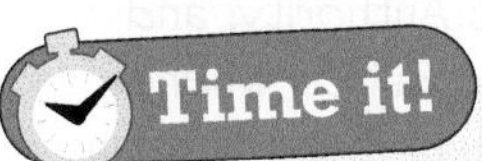

You do not need to spend much time on this question. You could allow around two minutes for your description.

Hint

When describing the features of business finance consider factors such as any initial upfront costs and fees, interest rates and repayment periods.

Hire purchase can be used as an alternative source of finance to leasing. Leasing involves acquiring the use of a non-current asset such as office equipment or machinery, and paying set payments over a fixed period, after which the asset is returned to the supplier.

Revision Guide page 58

Hint

For each advantage in this **explain** question, answer with a main point and then develop the point, for example debt counsellors help individuals prepare a personal budget plan to help them manage their finances.

Hint

A debt counsellor is authorised by the Financial Conduct Authority, and may be required when a person has failed to plan their budget and finances, and built up debt.

Explore

You also need to know the function, role and responsibilities, advantages and disadvantages of other sources of information, guidance and advice:

- Citizens Advice: a charity offering free advice
- Independent Financial Advisers (IFAs): offer professional financial advice for a fee
- Price comparison websites: provide access to interactive tools that can be personalised to meet needs of consumers wishing to purchase specific financial products, such as insurance.

3 Explain **two** advantages of using a debt counsellor.

1 ....

....

....

....

2 ....

....

....

....

Total for Question 3 = 4 mark

4 In 2013 a famous economist called Professor Angus Deaton stated in his book, *The Great Escape*, that 'Life is better now than at almost any time in history'. But try telling that to anyone aged between 21 and 35!

Discuss how the financial needs of a young adult differ from those of a pensioner.

....

....

....

....

....

....

....

....

....

....

....

....

Total for Question 4 = 6 marks

Hint

When answering this **discuss** question, consider different aspects of financial needs and how they differ between a young adult and a pensioner.

Hint

Financial needs relate to expenditure priorities and the ability to pay for them from savings or income. Consider savings and income from the perspective of a young person and an older person who may not have a significant income, though they may have pensions and savings.

Hint

Life stages and life events are factors that influence the difference between a young adult and a pensioner when managing personal finances. Other factors are personal attitudes, culture, interest rates and external influences.

The benefits of financial planning for all age groups are the ability to save and earn interest, a good credit rating and funding large purchases.

Revision Guide page 52

Hint

When answering this **assess** question, present a careful consideration of the options for Sarah and arrive at a conclusion.

Time it!

This assess question requires a longer answer that may take around 10 minutes. You may find it useful to plan your answer, dividing your time between the different options and your conclusion.

Hint

You need to match the requirements of the saver to the savings products. Consider the saver's personal circumstances, for example savings amount, access needed to savings. Weigh this against features of the saving products, for example rate of interest, access allowed, level of risk.

LEARN IT!

Corporate bonds are issued by public limited companies to raise finance. They pay investors regular interest over a set period, as long as the business is able to pay the interest.

5 Sarah is considering where to invest her recent £5000 Premium Bonds win. She is saving to buy a new car, which she plans to purchase after she passes her test.

Assess whether a variable instant access savings account or a fixed interest corporate bond would be better for Sarah.

....

....

....

....

....

....

....

....

....

....

....

....

....

....

....

....

....

....

....

....

....

....

Total for Question 5 = 10 marks

Davesh is a student who plays the guitar and electronic keyboard in local bars in his spare time to raise cash to support himself while studying. He has recently received good reviews in the local press after a performance.

He is looking to upgrade his musical equipment. A new guitar would cost around £700 and a new electronic keyboard around £1300.

Davesh charges £30 per evening and currently performs one or two evenings per week. Upgrading his equipment may result in additional bookings and increasing his booking fee.

He currently has savings of £200 to finance a business studies field trip on his course. The full cost is £600. He has opened a student bank account, which includes an interest-free overdraft of £500, and he has currently used £100 of this overdraft.

He is looking at different methods to finance the purchase of his new equipment.

This table gives information on products from different organisations.

Summary of finance products, and terms and conditions		
Provider	**Product**	**Features**
Ferris Bank	Current account	Interest-free overdraft of £500 Free tablet computer Overdraft fee 24.5%
Dialup Credit Ltd	Hire purchase	20% deposit with the balance repayable over one year 11.5% rate of interest
Clynedale Bank	Credit card	24.5% interest Credit limit £2000 3% cashback on all purchases
Capo Musical Instruments Ltd	Store card	21.5% rate of interest Credit limit £2500 10% discount on products purchased over £75

Revision Guide page 49–51

Hint

Read the **evaluate** question on the next page. You need to evaluate information about Davesh and information about different finance products, and come to a judgement about which is suitable.

Time it!

This evaluate question requires a longer answer that may take around 12–15 minutes. To help you evaluate given information, circle and underline key points to help plan your answer and allocate time.

Hint

Circle Davesh's **personal circumstances**. Underline his **financial circumstances**. Consider his income, commitments, savings and plans, and the risks of taking out a loan. Decide how each factor may affect his decision.

Watch out!

Some finance providers use additional benefits to attract customers. Davesh should not be swayed by these if it means he cannot afford future loan repayments.

Revision Guide
page 49–51

Hint

This question is based on the information on the previous page. Evaluate each product and the suitability of the financial products linked to Davesh's personal and financial circumstances. Use this to support your conclusion and recommendation.

Watch out!

Consider any associated risks. For example, Davesh does not have regular employment and may be relying on additional bookings.

Hint

Your evaluation might use some sentences that start as follows:

The decision of which financial product would be most suitable depends on Davesh's personal and financial circumstances...

An analysis of each financial product follows, matched to Davesh's personal and financial circumstances...

From this analysis I conclude that Davesh should prioritise a product that...

After considering all the financial products, I consider the most suitable provider would be...

The reason this product would be most suitable is because...

Evaluate which financial product would be most suitable for Davesh.

....

....

....

....

....

....

....

....

....

....

....

....

....

....

....

....

....

....

....

....

....

....

....

....

....

Total for Question 6 = 12 marks

TOTAL FOR SECTION A = 36 MARKS

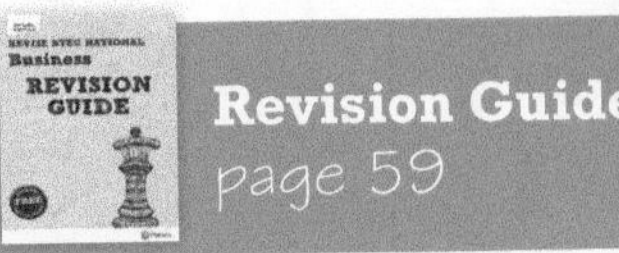

SECTION B: Business Finance

Answer ALL questions.
Write your answers in the spaces provided.

Ahmed owns a successful computer repair business in the town centre. The business will need to relocate to new premises as a result of the development of the town centre.

The owner of a retail computer shop, *Surf the Web*, has approached Ahmed to discuss the possibility of merging the two businesses together to form a partnership.

Ahmed has asked you to review a set of financial information sent to him by the accountant of *Surf the Web*, along with some information on his own business.

Identify **two** purposes of accounting.

1 ....

....

2 ....

....

Total for Question 7 = 2 marks

Revision Guide page 59

Time it!

When timing yourself to complete this practice assessment in two hours, spend around 75–80 minutes on Section B. Details of the actual assessment may change so check the latest guidance on the Pearson website to be sure you are up to date.

Hint

To answer this **identify** question you need to recall two purposes of Ahmed keeping accounts that are important for his business. You don't need to go into detail.

Explore

Some businesses do not keep thorough sets of accounts, and this can impact on their business efficiency and profitability. There are both advantages to keeping accounts, such as maintaining control and preventing fraud, but there are also disadvantages to keeping thorough sets of accounts such as the costs incurred.

Revision Guide pages 64 and 65

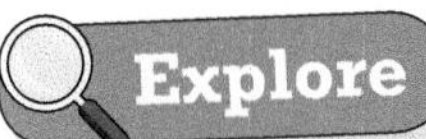

When answering **give** questions, you don't need to go into detail.

Watch out!

Only give examples of **external sources** of business finance. Don't include internal sources.

Explore

You also need to know about internal sources of finance:

- retained profit (kept in the business for reinvestment)
- net current assets (current assets + fixed assets – current liabilities)
- sale of assets (such as machinery to generate cash).

Explore

You also need to know short-term and long-term advantages and disadvantages of external and internal sources of finance, for example:

- external finance disadvantage: crowd-funding can be unreliable as funds promised are not always committed
- internal finance advantage: selling non-current assets if they are no longer needed.

8 Give **two** examples of external business finance.

1 ....

....

2 ....

....

Total for Question 8 = 2 marks

9 In January, Ahmed's business had trade payables of £12 500. They were all paid during January. During the month, goods costing £18 000 were purchased and, at the end of January, there was an amount of £13 600 owing to trade payables.

(a) Calculate the amount of cash paid to trade payables during January.

3 marks

Show your workings

£...

Revision Guide page 75

Hint

When answering a **calculate** question, you need to work out an answer by adding, multiplying, subtracting or dividing. This can involve the use of formulae.

You could spend around three minutes on this question. Extract the relevant figures and complete the calculation in stages.

Hint

Add together all payments and purchases made to trade payables in January and then subtract the amount still owing at the end of the month.

LEARN IT!

Trade payables is money owed by the business for goods it has bought on credit. Trade payables are current liabilities shown on the statement of financial position.

Explore

An analysis of trade payable days and trade receivable days can identify if a business has any potential cash flow problems.

Revision Guide page 79

Hint

Use the information in the table to assist you with the answer.

LEARN IT!

You need to use the following formulae for **trade payable days** and **trade receivable days**:

trade payable days = $\frac{\text{trade payables}}{\text{credit purchases}} \times 365$

trade receivable days = $\frac{\text{trade receivables}}{\text{credit sales}} \times 365$

LEARN IT!

Trade receivable days provide an indication of how long a business's customers take to pay their invoices and trade payable days provide an indication of how long a business takes to pay its suppliers' invoices.

Explore

The results from these ratios can indicate how efficient or inefficient a business is. For example, if the trade receivable days are too high then the cash flow in the business may suffer as a result.

Surf the Web has provided the following information.

Additional information	
Trade receivables	£4600
Trade payables	£11200
Credit sales	£87500
Credit purchases	£75980

(b) Calculate *Surf the Web*'s trade receivable days and trade payable days.

4 marks

Show your workings

inancial data for the most recent financial year presented by the owners of *urf the Web* is shown in the following table.

Financial data for *Surf the Web*	
Sales	£180 000
Opening inventory	£17 000
Closing inventory	£18 000
Rent	£8 400
Insurance	£1 880
Electricity	£1 920
Purchases	£105 250
Depreciation	£2 200

(c) Calculate the net profit for the year.

8 marks

Show your workings

£..

Revision Guide page 72

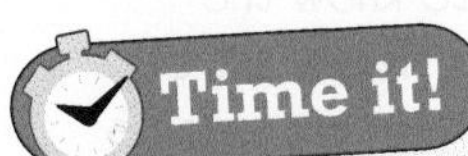

Hint

Make sure you include all the information in the table and complete the statement of comprehensive income in the correct order, ensuring gross profit before net profit.

Time it!

You could allow around eight minutes for this question that requires you to extract data from a table. You could use some of this time to double-check you have included all the correct figures from the table in your calculations.

Explore

The layout of the statement of comprehensive income is always the same, but sometimes some of the information contained in it may differ. For example, some expenses may change depending on the type of business. Not all businesses pay rent, as they may own the property.

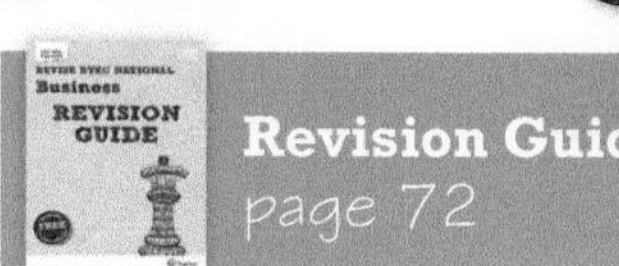

Revision Guide page 72

Hint

Arrears need to be subtracted and prepayments added to the figure for net profit.

LEARN IT!

You need to know the accounting treatment of accruals and prepayments and the impact that these can have on the financial statements. Prepayments occur when the business pays for something in advance and an accrual is an amount owing after using it, such as a phone bill.

Explore

You may be required to adjust financial statements to take account of accruals and prepayments. Both accruals and prepayments can occur on a number of different expenses and will have an impact on both the statement of comprehensive income and the statement of financial position.

As you review the paperwork provided by the owner of *Surf the Web* you discover that £525 for the year is still owed in electricity charges and £375 in insurance costs have been paid in advance.

(d) Calculate *Surf the Web*'s revised net profit.

3 marks

Show your workings

£..

Total for Question 9 = 18 marks

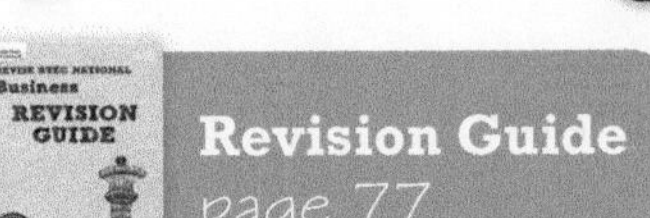

0 The owner of *Surf the Web* has invested £25 000 into the company to date and during the previous financial year withdrew £30 000 from the business as his salary.

(a) Calculate *Surf the Web*'s Return on Capital Employed (ROCE) using the figure for the revised net profit.

4 marks

Show your workings

Revision Guide page 77

Hint

Use the information provided in the question and the answer from Question 9d to calculate the answer.

LEARN IT!

The **capital employed** can be calculated by the following formula:

capital employed = owner's capital + retained profit − drawings

LEARN IT!

You need to know the following formula for the **Return on Capital Employed**:

$$\text{ROCE} = \frac{\text{net profit}}{\text{capital employed}} \times 100$$

Explore

If employed capital is not given in a question you can calculate it by subtracting current liabilities from total assets. In this case the **ROCE formula** would be:

$$\text{ROCE} = \frac{\text{net profit}}{\text{total assets} - \text{current liabilities}} \times 100$$

Revision Guide page 79

LEARN IT!

You need to know the formula for **inventory turnover**:

inventory turnover = $\frac{\text{average inventory}}{\text{cost of sales}} \times 365$

Average inventory can be calculated by the following formula:

average inventory = $\frac{\text{opening inventory + closing inventory}}{2}$

Time it!

Allow around two minutes for this question that requires you to extract figures from a table and insert them into a formula. Write out the formula first and then insert the figures in the second stage of your workings. Always double-check your calculation.

LEARN IT!

The figures for the opening inventory, the closing inventory and purchases can be used to calculate **the cost of sales** by using the following formula:

cost of sales = opening inventory + purchases − closing inventory

Hint

Before arriving at the final answer you will first need to calculate average inventory and costs of sales.

(b) Calculate *Surf the Web*'s inventory turnover using the table below, from Question 9c.

2 marks

Financial data for *Surf the Web*	
Sales	£180 000
Opening inventory	£17 000
Closing inventory	£18 000
Rent	£8 400
Insurance	£1 880
Electricity	£1 920
Purchases	£105 250
Depreciation	£2 200

Show your workings

Total for Question 10 = 6 marks

When looking through Ahmed's financial information you notice that he has experienced some cash flow issues. He is considering selling some of his non-current assets in order to improve the business's cash flow.

Discuss the potential impact on Ahmed's business if he decides to sell some of its non-current assets.

....

....

....

....

....

....

....

....

....

....

....

....

Total for Question 11 = 6 marks

Revision Guide
page 63, 73

Hint

This **discuss** question requires you to consider different aspects of the potential impact on Ahmed's business of selling his non-current assets. Consider how they interrelate and the extent to which they are important.

Hint

Non-current assets are included in the statement of financial position and include things such as machinery, plant and property. Some non-current assets will be subject to depreciation. Consider how selling some non-current assets could improve the business's liquidity – its ability to pay current liabilities.

Explore

You need to know the information included in the statement of financial position (assets, liabilities and capital) and how it can be used to assess the liquidity and performance of the business in terms of efficiency (inventory turnover) and returns (ROCE).

Revision Guide page 68

Hint

This **analyse** question requires you to present a detailed examination of the contribution of a cash flow forecast to the management and control of a business, but also the limitations of such a forecast.

Hint

When answering questions on financial statements use appropriate financial terminology. Here, use 'cash inflows', 'cash outflows' and 'net cash outflow'.

Hint

Consider why it would be useful for a business to know if there are any months where the business will have a net cash outflow and what could be done to manage and control the situation.

Watch out!

Cash flow forecasts are estimates, so it is likely that they will not be 100% accurate.

12 The financial information provided by the owner of *Surf the Web* contains a cash flow forecast for the next financial year. However, Ahmed is not convinced of the usefulness of such a forecast.

Analyse the use of a cash flow forecast in the management and control of business operations.

....

....

....

....

....

....

....

....

....

....

....

....

....

....

....

....

....

....

....

....

....

....

....

....

Total for Question 12 = 8 marks

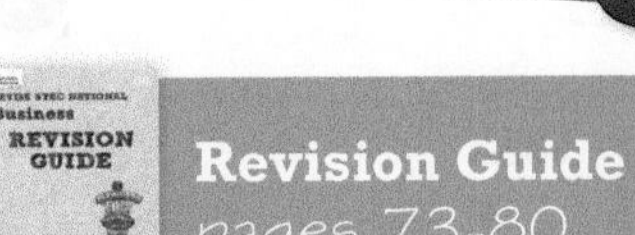

13 The information sent by *Surf the Web*'s owners includes its most recent financial statements. Ahmed understands the information contained in the statement of comprehensive income, but has always been less confident about how to interpret a statement of financial position.

Assess how *Surf the Web*'s statement of financial position could help Ahmed decide whether he should go into partnership with this business.

Total for Question 13 = 10 marks

Revision Guide pages 73-80

Hint

This question requires you to **assess** the information in the statement of financial position and how it can be used in ratio analysis to interpret the financial position of a business, and arrive at a conclusion.

Time it!

You could spend around 10 minutes on this assess question. You could make a brief plan and divide your time as you assess the information in the financial statement, and give an overview of the ratios and a conclusion.

Hint

Ratios can be calculated using the statement of financial position: current ratio, liquid capital ratio, inventory turnover, ROCE. Ratio analysis helps you to assess the financial health of a business and whether it is worth investing in.

Explore

Financial ratios such as profit margins and mark-up can also be derived from the statement of comprehensive income.

Revision Guide pages 76, 77, 79, 80

Hint

This **evaluate** question requires you to use the given ratios to consider the relative strengths and weaknesses of the business, and to comment on the usefulness and limitations of these ratios in determining business performance.

Watch out!

Don't confuse the terms gross and net profit with profit margins. The terms gross and net profit will be given in a monetary form, but gross profit margin will be expressed as a percentage.

Hint

A high turnover does not always mean a business is efficient. Different types of businesses have different levels of inventory turnover. The inventory turnover of a supermarket would be higher than a used car showroom as supermarkets have more customers buying more products.

Time it!

If you have time at the end of an assessment, check your answers and calculations.

14 Ahmed is keen to set performance targets for his business and, as part of the process, wants to focus on those areas where his business may be under-performing. He has calculated some financial ratios for his business, but has asked you how useful they are as a management tool.

Additional information	
Gross profit margin	22%
Net profit margin	8%
Inventory turnover	91 days

Evaluate the financial ratios supplied by Ahmed and comment on the limitations of such ratios when assessing business performance.

Total for Question 14 = 12 marks

TOTAL FOR SECTION B = 64 MARKS TOTAL FOR PAPER = 100 MARKS

Answers

Practice assessment 1

Use this section to check your answers.

- For questions with clear correct answers, these are provided. If there are alternative correct answers, these are given.
- For questions where answers may be individual or require longer answers, bullet points are provided to indicate key points you could include in your answer, or how your answer could be structured. **Your answer should be written using sentences and paragraphs**, and might include some of these points but not necessarily all of them.

The questions and sample answers are provided to help you revise content and skills. Ask your tutor or check the Pearson website for the most up-to-date Sample Assessment Material, past papers and mark schemes to get an indication of the actual assessment and what this requires of you. Details of the actual assessment may change so always make sure you are up to date.

SECTION A: Personal Finance

1 **Two** of the following:
- standard account
- packaged premium account
- student account
- basic account.

2 Individual responses. For example, **one** of the following points:
- This fund can pay compensation to consumers for financial loss if an authorised financial services business such as a bank or an insurance company fails.
- The FSCS covers claims against businesses authorised by the Financial Conduct Authority (FCA).

3 Individual responses. Points may include some of the below, for example:
- An increase in interest rates will reward savers with higher returns, which may mean they reduce their spending habits and increase the amount of money they save.
- An increase in interest rates will increase the cost of borrowing, which may mean people are less willing to take out loans to purchase expensive items such as cars and houses.

4 Individual responses. Your answer should show accurate and thorough knowledge and understanding of relevant information using specialist technical language, with a well-developed, balanced and logical discussion giving pros and cons.

Points may include some of the following, for example:
- Travel insurance is a financial service which provides compensation to the policyholder in relation to risks connected with travelling such as delayed flights, loss of holiday money, illness, loss of a passport and cancellation of travel arrangements.
- Temi needs to be aware of all the risks because, without travel insurance, she could suffer financial loss should any of these risks occur.
- Temi needs to take into account a number of factors that impact on the cost of travel insurance, which depend on her personal circumstances and the level of risk associated with them.
- Travel insurance will cost more if it applies to travel throughout the world. Temi is travelling to Europe so her insurance premium should be less.
- Travel insurance premiums will be higher if the compensation benefits are higher. Temi's holiday is likely to be relatively inexpensive and this should be reflected in her policy premium.
- Temi also needs to be aware that she might be required to pay a policy excess, in other words the amount of money she would pay towards a claim.
- If Temi does not make a claim on her travel insurance policy, her premium (the amount she paid for the policy) will not be returned to her.

5 Individual responses. Your answer should show accurate and thorough knowledge and understanding of relevant information using specialist technical language, with a well-developed, logical, balanced assessment that links and leads to a rational judgement.

Points may include some of the following, for example:

Advantages
- Life assurance is a long-term method of saving provided by life insurance companies.
- A life assurance policy provides the policyholder with two benefits – savings and a death benefit.
- The savings element involves the insurance company investing the policyholder's premiums into a range of investments such as shares. As a result, the money paid in premiums by the saver benefits from the dividends which accrue on the investments made on behalf of the policyholder by the insurance company.
- At the end of the policy term, the policyholder receives a lump sum based upon the value of their investment over time. This lump sum could be used to provide financial support to the policyholder's children when they enter higher education or to help reduce debt incurred by the student loan.
- The added advantage of a life assurance policy is that there will be a sum assured which is paid out in the event of the policyholder's death. The sum assured can be used to pay off personal debts such as a mortgage or be left to dependents.

Disadvantages
- A person using a life assurance policy as a method of saving should be aware that, whereas the sum assured in the event of death is guaranteed, the investment element is not guaranteed. This could mean that the purpose for the saving, for example supporting children so they do not have to rely so much on student loans, may not be met as intended.
- The policyholder could therefore receive less than the total amount of premiums they have paid in when the policy matures. This means they would have lost money.

Conclusion

Life assurance should be considered as part of a person's portfolio of financial products if they have dependents, have a mortgage, or wish to save for a long-term financial goal.

6 Individual responses. Your answer should show accurate and thorough knowledge and understanding of relevant information using specialist technical language. A well-developed, balanced evaluation should draw on links and interrelationships between the factors with a grasp of competing arguments and logical reasoning leading to supported conclusions.

When reading the information with the question you should have established the following relevant information to inform your evaluation:

Personal circumstances

Young couple, currently renting, no children, seeking to buy property.

Financial circumstances

Savings: joint ISA with deposit saved of £70 000.

Income: Simon £19 000; Deepa £25 000; joint income: £44 000.

Purchase price of flat: £200 000.

Costs of move: solicitor fixed fee £2000.

Other factors

Future career prospects and potential earnings:

Simon: trainee accountant so income likely to increase when fully qualified.

Deepa: works in local company so may not have same career opportunities as Simon, who works for a multinational company.

Potential for future family and effect on financial circumstances:

Family income and expenditure may be affected if Deepa or Simon do not return to work or go part-time; if Simon leaves his job to look after the children or works from home as an accountant; if childcare needs to be funded.

Calculation of mortgage required

Deposit available: £70 000 minus £2000 solicitor fees = £68 000

Mortgage required: £132 000 (£200 000 for cost of flat minus £68 000 deposit from savings).

You could use the sentence starters in the hint box on page 7 as you evaluate and link the above and below points.

Points may include some of the following, for example:

- Three out of the four mortgage providers will offer a mortgage of £132 000 or more.
- Audley Building Society do not offer a large enough mortgage, so ignore this mortgage provider.
- Brimsdown Building Society offers the lowest fixed rate cost but only for five years, after which it reverts to a variable rate.
- Central Bank offers the highest interest rate, but it is fixed for the period of the loan, which allows for easier budgeting. Also, over time, if general interest rates rise, the fixed rate may become lower than the variable rate. In addition, if their income increases it will not be such a strain on their budget.
- Danesland Bank offers the lowest variable cost, but this will rise or fall in line with the general rate of interest.
- The decision will largely depend on Simon and Deepa's attitude towards risk. A variable interest rate mortgage may be less than the fixed rate, but it may increase during the mortgage period. It may therefore be that a fixed interest rate from Central Bank will be more suitable, as although monthly payments are higher, it is a fixed rate for the period of the loan and may allow for more effective budgeting of the household income.

SECTION B: Business Finance

7 Individual responses. For example, **two** of the following:

- inventory
- rent
- rates
- heating and lighting
- water
- insurance
- administration
- telephone/internet charges
- postage
- stationery
- salaries
- wages
- marketing
- bank charges
- interest paid
- straight-line depreciation
- reducing balance depreciation
- discount allowed.

8 Individual responses. For example:

- The outline should include a definition:
  - A non-current asset is an asset that the business has purchased and expects to keep in the business for more than one year.
- The outline should include an example or a further fact:
  - Examples are property or equipment.
  - Non-current assets, such as machinery and equipment, may depreciate in value over time.

9(a)

A: Total cash outflows (Feb) = £900 + £250 + £225 + £300 = £1675.

B: Net cash inflow (outflow) (March) = £5000 – £2120 = £2880.

C: Interest payments (April) = £4595 – (£2400 + £620 + £700 + £800) = £4595 – £4520 = £75.

9(b)

Opening balance for May = £11 210.

Net cash inflow (outflow) for May = £11 300 – £12 200 = (£900).

Closing balance for May = opening balance +/– net cash inflow (outflow).

Closing balance for May = £11 210 – £900 = £10 310.

9(c)

Projected Statement of Comprehensive Income		
	£	£
Sales	75 800	
Cost of sales	49 649	
Gross profit		**26 151**
Business expenses		
Rent	12 000	
Advertising	200	
Insurance	422	
Heating and lighting	1 250	
Transport	1 450	
Loan interest	675	
Printing	745	
Office supplies	1 450	
Total expenses		**18 192**
Net profit		**7 959**

9(d)

$$\text{Gross profit margin} = \frac{26\,151}{75\,800} \times 100 = 34.5\%$$

$$\text{mark-up} = \frac{26\,151}{49\,649} \times 100 = 52.67\%$$

$$\text{Net profit margin} = \frac{7959}{75\,800} \times 100 = 10.5\%$$

10(a)

Total assets are made up of inventory + delivery van + cash balances = £8000

Total assets = £1000 + £2500 + cash balances = £8000
Cash balances = £8000 – (£1000 + £2500)
= £8000 – £3500
= £4500

Current assets = inventory + cash balances
= £1000 + £4500
= £5500

Cash liabilities = total liabilities – non-current liabilities
= £4500 – £2000
= £2500

$$\text{Liquid capital ratio} = \frac{\text{current assets} - \text{inventory}}{\text{current liabilities}}$$

$$= \frac{5500 - 1000}{2500}$$

$$= \frac{4500}{2500}$$

$$= 1.8{:}1$$

10b

Value of delivery van at the end of Year 1 = £2500 – (10% of £2500)
= £2500 – £250
= £2250

Value of delivery van at the end of Year 2 = £2250 – (10% of £2250)
= £2250 – £225
= £2025

11 Individual responses. Your answer should show accurate and thorough knowledge and understanding of relevant information using specialist technical language, with a well-developed, balanced and logical discussion considering different aspects of the topic.

Points may include some of the following, for example.

Cash flow forecasts:

- can be a useful tool to identify the planned cash inflows and outflows into and out of a business
- can allow potential cash flow problems to be identified and actions put in place to address net cash outflows
- are forecasts or assumptions about future cash inflows and cash outflows – if the assumptions on which the forecasts are made are not correct, this could seriously impact a business decision (for example, sales may not meet the expectations of the business or costs may rise due to external factors such as inflation)
- must be accurate, and many businesses omit to include some costs resulting in potential cash flow difficulties over time
- are particularly difficult for new business start-ups who may not have a track record in financial planning
- can become outdated very quickly and won't necessarily take changes into consideration (for example, the forecast will assume all customers pay on time and in full – if allowance is not made, this could impact on the liquidity of the business).

12 Individual responses. Your answer should show accurate and thorough knowledge and understanding of relevant information using specialist technical language. The balanced analysis should contain linkages and interrelationships between factors, showing logical reasoning.

Points may include some of the following, for example.

Break-even analysis:

- is a planning tool which enables a business to calculate the level of sales required to break even (the level of sales above which the business will start to make a profit)
- enables the business to calculate the contribution made by each sale towards covering its fixed costs, through analysing the structure of its costs and identifying its fixed, variable and semi-variable costs
- is based upon the principles of contribution. Contribution per unit can be calculated by subtracting the variable price per unit from the selling price, in other words selling price – fixed costs per unit. This can then be used to calculate the number of units required to be sold in order to break even by the formula:

$$\frac{\text{fixed costs}}{\text{contribution}}$$

- can assist the business in calculating its margin of safety (the amount of unit sales above the break-even point)
- helps the business to identify the impact of changes in prices and costs on the break-even point and to set a price that will enable it to make a profit
- alerts the business to take action if costs rise or if there is a fall in sales – both of which will increase the break-even point and reduce the margin of safety
- helps the business to set SMART targets for sales and costs which will help it meet its target profit level
- should be used with some caution as it is based on the idea that cost and revenue lines are perfectly straight when plotted against volume of output – this may not be the case in real life (for example fixed costs may increase over a certain level of activity; or if a business is producing lots of different products it may be difficult to separate out the fixed costs between the different products).

13 Individual responses. Your answer should show accurate and thorough knowledge and understanding of relevant information using specialist technical language, with a well-developed, logical, balanced assessment that links and leads to a rational judgement.

Points may include some of the following, for example:

- Leasing and hire purchase are both methods of finance that can be used by a business to acquire non-current assets such as machinery and equipment. There are advantages and disadvantages to each method of finance.
- Hire purchase requires the business to pay a deposit, usually a percentage of the purchase price. The outstanding balance is then paid off in regular instalments which include interest payments. The equipment is then owned by the business once all the payments have been made.
- Leasing is similar to renting. The business does not own the non-current asset and pays regular amounts, usually monthly, to the leasing company for a set period of time after which the non-current asset is returned to the leasing company. Some leasing arrangements may include an option to buy at the end of the leasing period.
- In the short-term, hire purchase may be more expensive due to the interest element and the initial cash deposit may deplete the business's cash reserves and cause liquidity problems. In addition, in the long-term, at the end of the hire purchase agreement, depreciation will result in a fall in value of the asset.
- Under a leasing arrangement, the asset can be returned and replaced by a more up to date, and potentially more productive, piece of equipment. This is particularly useful for those non-current assets such as computers and office equipment which can be improved as a result of advances in technology. Such equipment purchased on hire purchase may become quickly outdated. Hence, in the long-term, leasing may be a better option than hire purchase for these types of non-current assets.
- Overall, Raj's decision should be based upon whether he wants to own the equipment outright (in which case he should choose hire purchase) or whether he wants to upgrade the equipment on a regular basis (in which case leasing is the better option).

14 Individual responses. Your answer should show accurate and thorough knowledge and understanding of relevant information using specialist technical language. The well-developed, balanced evaluation should draw on linkages and interrelationships between the factors with a grasp of competing arguments and logical reasoning leading to supported conclusions.

Points may include some of the following, for example:

Trade payable days

- This is the average number of days for the business to pay its suppliers – businesses with cash flow problems are likely to take the longest to pay.
- In Raj's case, his trade payable days are 54 days which means that, on average, his business is taking 54 days to pay.

- The competitor's trade payable days are 40 days which means that they are paying their suppliers more quickly than Raj.
- This could mean that Raj has cash flow problems and is unable to pay his suppliers on time, which could impact on his business relationship with his suppliers, who may not be willing to supply him with products unless he settles his bills within the trade credit period.
- This could result in establishing a competitive advantage for his competitor – for example, suppliers may offer more favourable credit terms.

Trade receivable days

- This is the average length of time trade receivables take to pay their invoices.
- In Raj's case, his trade receivable days are 60 days which means that, on average, his trade receivables are taking 60 days to pay.
- If Raj's business offers trade credit terms of 30 days, then the business may have issues with its credit control systems and if credit control is weak this may result in cash flow difficulties (as evidenced by the high trade payables days).
- This compares unfavourably with the competitor whose trade receivables days are 31 days, so the customers settle their bills twice as fast as Raj's customers.
- This could result in a competitive advantage for his competitor, with a positive impact on cash flow.

Inventory turnover

- On average, Raj's inventory has a life of 28 days compared to the local competitor's inventory turnover of 18 days.
- The relatively high level of inventory turnover is linked to the fact that both businesses are dealing with food products which need to be replenished on a regular basis.
- Raj's business re-orders inventory on average 13 times a year, whereas the local competitor re-orders inventory 20 times a year – this could mean that Raj's inventory management systems are not as efficient as his competitor, which could result in higher costs as a result of an increase in wastage.

Conclusion

On the basis of these figures, Raj is not efficient and he needs to take steps to:

- reduce trade payables days
- reduce trade receivables days – if this figure can be reduced, it may have a beneficial knock-on effect on Raj's ability to pay his suppliers, thereby reducing his trade payables days
- improve inventory management within the business to reduce the possibility of wastage.

Practice assessment 2

SECTION A: Personal Finance

1 **Two** of the following, for example:
- life stages
- culture
- life events
- external influences
- interest rates
- attitudes towards risk and reward.

2 **Two** of the following, for example:
- issued by retailers
- can only be used in issuer's stores
- rate of interest charged on outstanding balances
- cardholders may benefit from discounts
- cardholders may benefit from loyalty schemes.

3 Individual responses. Points may include some of the following, for example:
- Customers manage their accounts remotely through a mobile device such as a smartphone or tablet, which means they can transact and pay bills without visiting the bank in person.
- Customers can access accounts at any time, day or night, with the advantage that banking is faster and more efficient.

4 Individual responses. Your answer should show accurate and thorough knowledge and understanding of relevant information using specialist technical language, with a well-developed, balanced and logical discussion giving pros and cons.
Points may include some of the following, for example:

Pros

- Building societies are specialist financial institutions providing two main types of financial products – savings accounts, and short- and long-term loans such as mortgages that can be used to purchase property.
- For many people, owning their house is a long-term ambition, yet many will not have the financial resources to pay for a property outright. Their long-term financial target will be to save for a deposit, then take out a mortgage for the remainder of the amount they require.
- Building societies can help potential home owners by offering a range of savings accounts, including easy access and fixed rate accounts. Savers can deposit money into their accounts on a regular basis and, when they have saved a sufficient amount of money to put a deposit on a house, they can apply to their building society for a mortgage, which can be paid back monthly over a long period of time – in many cases in excess of 20 years.
- Building societies historically offer a better rate of interest to savers as they do not have to pay dividends to shareholders and usually have lower overheads than banks. This would benefit the long-term financial plan for a customer.
- They traditionally have offered cheaper mortgages than banks, so a customer would pay less back over the course of the mortgage.
- Building society savings accounts can also be used by those people whose long-term financial targets include saving for holidays, high cost items such as cars, or putting money aside for their retirement.

Cons

- Building societies do not always offer the full range of services that banks do. This may have an impact on the long-term targets for customers who may wish to use a variety of financial products as part of their plan.
- Building societies do not always have the same range of online services or number of branches as they try to keep their overheads down to offer better rates of interest to savers.

5 Individual responses. Your answer should show accurate and thorough knowledge and understanding of relevant information using specialist technical language, with a well-developed, logical, balanced assessment that links and leads to a rational judgement.
Points may include some of the following, for example:

Features of credit cards

- Credit cards are issued by banks and other financial institutions.
- They allow the credit card holder to use the card to pay for goods and services up to a set amount of credit.
- The credit card holder is required to either pay off the whole amount they have spent using their credit card each month or pay a minimum amount set by the credit card company.
- The credit card allows individuals to purchase goods on credit that they would otherwise not be able to afford and then pay the borrowed amount over time in monthly payments.
- The credit card issuer allows the individual a length of time before payments have to be made towards the outstanding balance on the credit card.

Advantages of credit cards in personal budgeting

- They give instant access to additional funds in times of emergency.

- Credit cards can have interest-free periods that apply to purchases and cash transfers, allowing customers to have interest-free loans for specific time periods.
- They allow you to manage your personal cash flow better.
- Using credit cards responsibly can maintain and build a good credit rating.
- They offer certain types of legal protection against the products that you buy.

Disadvantages of credit cards in personal budgeting

- Given their convenience, an individual may be tempted to purchase goods they cannot afford.
- If not paying off the balance outstanding at the end of each month, the amount of interest owed will increase over time.
- Credit cards can be difficult in personal budgets if the credit card holder is tempted to use the credit card even though the outstanding balance continues to increase each month, resulting in financial difficulties in the long-run.

Conclusion

- Credit cards are a useful source of obtaining personal credit as they are convenient and, if used wisely, can result in interest-free credit for an individual.
- Care must be taken that they are used sensibly so that the money borrowed on credit can be paid back.

6 Individual responses. Your answer should show accurate and thorough knowledge and understanding of relevant information using specialist technical language. The well-developed, balanced evaluation should draw on linkages and interrelationships between the factors with a grasp of competing arguments and logical reasoning leading to supported conclusions.

> When reading the information with the question you should have established the following relevant information to inform your evaluation:
>
> **Personal circumstances:** Mrs Foster is recovering from knee surgery (so need to consider potential risk when abroad or that the holiday may have to be cancelled altogether due to complications).
>
> **Financial circumstances:** Holiday costs £5000; one holiday per year (annual) – do not require multi-trip; Spanish holiday – do not require 'worldwide cover'; holiday money of £200.
>
> You could use the sentence starters in the hint box on page 26 as you evaluate and link the above and below points.

Points may include some of the following, for example:

- ProAchieve Insurers offers good value for money (lowest cost/multi-trip) but only covers cancellation up to £4000 (Foster family's holiday cost £5000); travel delay is the lowest at £5 per day; high excess baggage delay.
- Shales Insurance Services is the most expensive (£425), but cancellation cover is £5000 (however the excess is £400, which means the Fosters would only receive £4600 in the event of cancellation). Personal money is up to £2000 (not required by the Fosters who only take £200 in cash). Includes paying for worldwide cover which is not required.
- Laminster Insurance Ltd offers cancellation cover of £3000 (below that required by the Foster family). Hospital daily benefit is £100 per day (may be useful due to the risk associated with Mrs Foster's recent knee surgery).
- Therefore, I would recommend Expeditions Insurance Limited because all the family needs are met reasonably, as their offer includes cancellation cover of £5250 with £150 excess (meets the requirements of the family). Personal money covered is £500 (more than required but meets requirements). Hospital benefit is £50 per day (reasonable). Holiday interruption covered is £2000 (reasonable).

SECTION B: Business Finance

7 **Two** of the following:

- cash
- inventory
- bank account deposits
- trade receivables
- prepayments.

8 Individual responses. Points may include one of the below, for example:

- A cash flow forecast will enable Bilal to estimate the monthly cash inflows and cash outflows with his business in order to identify those months where there is a net cash outflow.
- A cash flow forecast will enable Bilal to predict if his business is likely to experience cash flow problems, so he can plan for any unexpected bills or payments, ensuring his business has enough cash to survive.

9(a)

(i) Total assets = current assets + non-current assets
= £8000 + £7250
= £15 250

(ii) $\text{Current ratio} = \dfrac{\text{current assets}}{\text{current liabilities}}$

$= \dfrac{8000}{2000}$

$= 4:1$

(iii) $\text{Liquid capital ratio} = \dfrac{\text{current assets} - \text{inventory}}{\text{current liabilities}}$

$= \dfrac{8000 - 2000}{2000}$

$= \dfrac{6000}{2000}$

$= 3:1$

9(b)

$\text{Annual depreciation charge} = \dfrac{\text{asset purchase price} - \text{estimated salvage value}}{\text{estimated useful life of the asset}}$

$= \dfrac{£4000 - £500}{4 \text{ years}}$

$= \dfrac{£3500}{4 \text{ years}}$

= £875 per year

Year 1 net book value = £4000 – £875 = £3125
Year 2 net book value = £3125 – £875 = £2250
Year 3 net book value = £2250 – £875 = £1375
Year 4 net book value = £1375 – £875 = £500

> The final net book value should equal the salvage value, in this case £500.

9(c)

It is known that the gross profit margin is 20%, therefore gross profit (A) is 20% of £96 000 = £19 200.
Now (B) + (A) £19 200 = £96 000 so that (B) is the difference. In other words, £76 800.
Now that (B) is known, (C) can be deduced: £88 200 – (C) = £76 800. So (C) is the difference, in other words £11 400.
We know that gross profit is £19 200 and, since the figure for net profit is given as £12 900, we can deduce that expenses (D) are £19 200 – £12 900 = £6300.

9(d)

$$\text{Inventory turnover} = \frac{\text{average inventory}}{\text{cost of sales}} \times 365$$

where $$\text{average inventory} = \frac{\text{opening inventory} + \text{closing inventory}}{2}$$

$$= \frac{£19\,500 + £11\,400}{2}$$

$$= \frac{£30\,900}{2}$$

$$= £15\,450$$

$$\text{Inventory turnover} = \frac{\text{average inventory}}{\text{cost of sales}} \times 365$$

$$= \frac{15\,450}{76\,800} \times 365$$

$$= 73.4 \text{ days}$$

> Show your workings for each stage of your calculations as marks may be given for correct workings.

10(a)

$$\text{Break-even point} = \frac{\text{fixed costs}}{\text{contribution per unit}}$$

where contribution per unit = selling price per unit − variable cost per unit

$$\text{Break-even point} = \frac{2000}{20 - 12}$$

$$= \frac{2000}{8}$$

$$= 250 \text{ units}$$

10(b)

$$\text{Months to break even} = \frac{\text{break-even units}}{\text{units produced per month}}$$

Production is 1152 units per year, in other words $\frac{1152 \text{ units}}{12 \text{ months}}$ = 96 units per month

So months to break even = $\frac{250}{96}$ = 2.6 months (or just over two and a half months)

11 Individual responses. Your answer should show accurate and thorough knowledge and understanding of relevant information using specialist technical language, with a well-developed, balanced and logical discussion giving pros and cons.

Points may include some of the following, for example:

- Accountants are professionally qualified financial specialists who can provide a number of important financial services and functions to a small business.
- Accountants can help a business to plan their business activities by helping to prepare cash flow forecasts and business plans which can be presented to banks when applying for loan finance.
- An accountant can record transactions and track trade receivables and trade payables to enhance the financial controls within the business so that the business does not get into financial difficulties.
- For small businesses an accountant is of prime importance in preparing the main financial statements – the statement of comprehensive income and the statement of financial position in accordance with legal requirements.
- The accountant can analyse the main financial statements to report on business performance and suggest areas which should be targeted for improvement.

12 Individual responses. Your answer should show accurate and thorough knowledge and understanding of relevant information using specialist technical language. The balanced analysis should contain linkages and interrelationships between factors, showing logical reasoning.

Points may include some of the following, for example:

- Depreciation is a charge made against the value of non-current assets which recognises that their value over time will be reduced as a result of factors such as wear and tear. A piece of equipment may be subject to break-down and a company vehicle may lose its value as a result of mileage. As a non-current asset influences the value of a business, depreciation reflects the fact that the market value of non-current assets may fall over time.
- Depreciation can be calculated either by the straight-line method (which subtracts a set amount from the value of the non-current asset each year) or by the reducing balance method (which subtracts a set percentage from the value of the non-current asset each year). In both cases the figure arrived at for the non-current asset will be its net book value, which will be the figure that is recorded in the statement of financial position.
- It can be seen from this analysis therefore that depreciation is a business expense and like all business expenses it must be shown in the statement of comprehensive income along with other expenses such as advertising, wages and utilities. These expenses are subtracted from the business's gross profit to arrive at the business's net profit.
- The value of a non-current asset when purchased and the depreciation for that year will be shown in the statement of financial position. The non-current asset will be reduced by the depreciation for that year, leaving the net book value being the current value of the non-current asset. The depreciation charge for that year will then be recorded in the statement of comprehensive income under 'business expenses'.

13 Individual responses. Your answer should show accurate and thorough knowledge and understanding of relevant information using specialist technical language, with a well-developed, logical, balanced assessment that links and leads to a rational judgement.

Points may include some of the following, for example:

- **Internal sources of finance** that Bilal may consider to support the development of the business could include using net current assets, retained profits or selling off some of his inventory.
- Net current assets involve using current cash reserves or selling off some of his inventory. Using cash reserves is relatively straightforward but could result in cash flow difficulties in the future. Selling off part of the inventory may mean having to accept a lower price than he anticipated, which could impact upon his cash flow forecast. The overall impact could be a reduction in net current assets, which may mean that the business is unable to meet its current liabilities.
- Using retained profits has the advantage of no interest being payable, but for a small business retained profits may not be large enough to meet requirements.
- Selling off non-current assets such as vehicles and equipment is useful to dispose of out-of-date equipment and will increase cash inflows, but they may need replacing in the future.
- Any one of the above methods would be suitable for Bilal to use to enable his future plans as they do not incur interest. All of the above methods have their own drawbacks and Bilal needs to consider whether the overall gain to the business is worth more than the drawbacks.

- **External sources of finance** could include leasing or hire purchase, bank loans and trade credit. Leasing, hire purchase and bank loans will all result in additional costs to the business. Bank loans and hire purchase for example, will incur interest charges and leasing will result in additional monthly outlays.
- Leasing may be particularly useful to Bilal because he will be able to access up-to-date equipment such as computers and other technology equipment, which he can return (and then update) at the end of the leasing period.
- This is not the case with hire purchase, which will also require an initial deposit (reducing cash reserves).
- Bank loans will incur interest charges, but will not result in an immediate reduction in cash reserves. Bilal could purchase equipment outright using the loan and may secure a discount for a cash purchase.
- Trade credit is useful for revenue expenditure on stock, components and raw materials. Suppliers will give 30 days (or more) trade credit – essentially a 'buy now, pay later' arrangement which does not incur interest charges. This will allow Bilal the opportunity to generate sales in order to pay for supplies after the end of the 30 days.
- **Conclusion:** After assessing the different sources of finance, and the costs he will incur as part of his plan, the recommendation is that Bilal should lease any equipment and computer hardware initially to allow him to set up his business plan more quickly and with the least risk. He might wish to use either a loan or retained profits to pay for any software development and website changes he needs to allow for his plan to be implemented.

14 Individual responses. Your answer should show accurate and thorough knowledge and understanding of relevant information using specialist technical language. The well-developed, balanced evaluation should draw on linkages and interrelationships between the factors with a grasp of competing arguments and logical reasoning leading to supported conclusions.
Points may include some the following, for example:

- **Current ratio:** This is a measure of a business's liquidity, in other words the ability of the business to meet its current liabilities. *Bilal's Bikes* is in a better position than *Wally's Wheels* because the former has £1.75 in current assets to meet every £1 of current liabilities, whereas *Wally's Wheels* only has £1.53 of assets for every £1 of current liabilities (although this measure includes the inventory, which is a less liquid current asset).
- **Mark-up:** This measures the percentage increase in the cost of sales which generates the gross profit of the business. The mark-up for *Bilal's Bikes* is 25% and for *Wally's Wheels* is 30%. There appears to be more potential for *Wally's Wheels* to make a larger gross profit than *Bilal's Bikes*, although this does depend on local market conditions.
- **ROCE:** This is the return on capital employed. The owner of *Wally's Wheels* receives a higher return on investment than *Bilal's Bikes* (7% as opposed to 5%). ROCE can be improved by increasing net profit (reviewing costs) or selling off unwanted non-current assets (so that the capital employed is reduced).
- **Trade payables:** This is the average number of days for the business to pay its suppliers. *Wally's Wheels* pays its bills on time (assuming 30 days trade credit). *Bilal's Bikes* takes longer to pay (could be a control issue or a cash flow issue).
- **Trade receivables:** This is the average number of days trade receivables take to pay their invoices. *Wally's Wheels* trade receivables take 37 days to pay their invoices (assuming 30 days trade credit, this should be tightened up). *Bilal's Bikes* trade receivables take even longer to pay their invoices (42 days). Both businesses need to review their credit control procedures and follow up trade receivables (*Wally's Wheels* may also be experiencing cash flow problems).
- **Conclusion:** *Bilal's Bikes* is in a better position in relation to liquidity, but is in a less favourable position in terms of mark-up, ROCE, trade payables and trade receivables. This shows that much work needs to be done by the owner of *Bilal's Bikes* in order to match the performance of a similar business.

Practice assessment 3

SECTION A: Personal Finance

1 **Two** of the following, for example:
- to avoid getting into debt
- to control costs
- to avoid legal action and/or repossession
- to remain solvent
- to maintain a good credit rating
- to avoid bankruptcy
- to manage money to fund purchases
- to generate income/savings
- to set financial targets and goals
- to provide insurance against loss or illness
- to counter the effects of inflation.

2 **Two** of the following, for example:
- fee charged to the account holder
- offers benefits such as discounts/special offers on goods and services
- offers interest on credit balances
- offers cashback on household bills or other purchases
- offers preferential terms on credit arrangements
- offers benefits such as insurance and breakdown cover.

3 Individual responses. Points may include some of the following, for example:
- The FCA regulates the conduct of financial service providers such as banks and insurance companies, by authorising them to offer financial services.
- The FCA monitors the conduct of financial service providers once they have received authorisation to offer financial services to customers and can stop businesses offering services if they are shown to be working against the interest of consumers.

4 Individual responses. Your answer should show accurate and thorough knowledge and understanding of relevant information using specialist technical language, with a well-developed, balanced and logical discussion giving pros and cons.
Points may include some of the following, for example:

Benefits
- A person buying shares in a public limited company becomes part-owner of that company. As one of the owners of the company they may receive a share of the profits in the form of a share dividend.
- The size of a dividend will depend on the number of shares held by the individual. Shareholders will vote on the size of the dividend to be paid each year at the company's Annual General Meeting.
- If the company is profitable, shares may increase in value and the individual can sell them on the Stock Exchange. If the business goes bankrupt, the shareholder will only lose the amount of money they have invested in the company. They will not have to sell their personal possessions.

Drawbacks
- Dividends on shares are not guaranteed. Circumstances may arise when, even if the company makes a profit, the shareholder will not receive a dividend, for example the business may decide to retain all the profits for future investment in the business. The value of shares can also fall, resulting in a fall in the value of the shareholders' personal wealth.

- Shares are a long-term investment that are primarily suitable for those individuals who are willing to take the risk that the value of their investments could either increase or decrease.

5 Individual responses. Your answer should show accurate and thorough knowledge and understanding of relevant information using specialist technical language, with a well-developed, logical, balanced assessment that links and leads to a rational judgement.

Points may include some of the following, for example:

Features of online banking

- Online banking allows account holders to manage their bank accounts using a computer, tablet or smartphone.
- Account holders using the service will be required to set up a security password which should not be divulged to third parties.

Advantages of online banking

- Allows the customer 24/7 access to their account so that they can check the balance on their account, pay bills and transfer money between different accounts.
- Convenient for customers as they do not have to visit the bank in person.

Disadvantages of online banking

- Accounts may be subject to 'hacking' (being stolen) by third parties, resulting in inconvenience and financial loss.
- Security may be compromised if the account holder divulges their password to someone else.
- Banking services are limited, for example an account holder cannot deposit cash into their account using online banking and some prefer a personal service from assistants in banks.
- Requires access to a computer which may be an additional cost to the individual.
- Requires computer skills that not all customers possess.

Conclusion

- Overall, although some banking services are not available via online banking, online access is more convenient and allows the customer a wide range of services.
- Most banks provide online access and it is becoming more widely used, therefore it is better to have online access.

6 Individual responses. Your answer should show accurate and thorough knowledge and understanding of relevant information using specialist technical language. The well-developed, balanced evaluation should draw on linkages and interrelationships between the factors with a grasp of competing arguments and logical reasoning leading to supported conclusions.

> When reading the information given with the question, you should have established the following to inform your evaluation:
>
> **Personal circumstances**
>
> Need to set aside £1500 in 12 months' time for incidental services, such as photographer, entertainer.
>
> Need access to £1800 savings in 18 months' time for payment of deposit on hotel, six months in advance of the wedding.
>
> **Financial circumstances**
>
> Wedding cost: £20 000.
>
> Have been given £10 000, therefore require an additional £10 000.
>
> You could use the sentence starters in the hint box on page 45 as you evaluate and link the above and below points.

Points may include some of the following, for example:

- Savings available:
  - £10 000 can be saved for one year (no access required) then £1500 payment for incidental services is required
  - £8500 (plus any interest gained) can be saved for a further six months then £1800 payment for deposit on the hotel is required
  - £6700 (plus any interest gained) can be saved for the remaining six months before their wedding takes place.
- Overall savings plan could be to save £10 000 in a fixed interest rate account for one year, then put the accumulated savings into a variable account for the remaining 12 months.
- Exmouth Building Society has an interest rate of 1.6% fixed for a year (ISA).
- Clynedale Bank offers a higher interest rate (1.7%), but this is only for 6 months, when it then reduces to 0.7%.
- Premium Bonds are probably not an option for relatively short-term savings plans. They are better suited to those people who can afford to set aside funds which are not required over the long term. Access to the funds is limited and arrangements would have to be made to redeem ('cash in') the Premium Bonds. There is also no guarantee of any financial return on the investment.
- Ferris Bank has an interest rate of 1.25% which is currently lower than either Exmouth Building Society or Ferris Bank, but if this rate was to be maintained in 12 months' time it would offer the highest interest rate of the three financial institutions. However, the £8500 (+ interest) could then be transferred from Exmouth Building Society to Ferris Bank allowing for instant access. The 3% cashback might be useful to pay for wedding expenses, although care should be taken regarding the interest payments on outstanding credit card balances.

SECTION B: Business Finance

7 **Two** of the following, for example:

cash sales, credit sales, discounts received, interest received, commission received, rent received.

8 Individual responses. Points may include one of the following, for example:

- Trade credit enables a business to purchase goods, for example raw materials and components from a supplier, and pay for them at a later date, such as 30 days' time, so the business can sell the goods and then use the revenue from the sales to pay the supplier when the credit period ends.
- If a business has purchased raw materials on trade credit from a supplier then it can manufacture goods using these raw materials thereby enabling continuous production to take place and limiting any cash flow problems.

9(a)

Gross profit = £42 000 – £16 800 = £25 200

$$\text{Gross profit margin} = \frac{\text{gross profit}}{\text{sales}} \times 100$$

$$= \frac{25\,200}{42\,000} \times 100$$

$$= 60\%$$

Net profit = gross profit – expenses
= £25 200 – (£1250 + £870 + £7200 + £10 000)
= £25 200 –£19 320
= £5880

$$\text{Net profit margin} = \frac{\text{net profit}}{\text{sales}} \times 100$$

$$= \frac{5880}{42\,000} \times 100$$

$$= 14\%$$

> Show your workings for each stage of your calculations as marks may be given for correct workings even if the answer is incorrect.

9(b)

Current forecast cost of sales = £16 800
5% increase in £16 800 = £840
Revised cost of sales = £16 800 + £840 = £17 640
Revised gross profit = £42 000 – £17 640 = £24 360

$$\text{Mark-up} = \frac{\text{gross profit}}{\text{cost of sales}} \times 100$$

$$= \frac{24\,360}{17\,640} \times 100$$

$$= 138\%$$

9(c)

Statement of financial position		
	£	£
Non-current assets		
Gym equipment	2 400	
Motor vehicles	1 200	3 600
Current assets		
Inventory	1 400	
Cash in bank	650	
Trade receivables	1 350	3 400
TOTAL ASSETS		**7 000**
Current liabilities		
Trade payables	400	
TOTAL LIABILITIES		**400**
Owner's capital and retained profit		
Owner's capital	720	
Profit	5 880	
TOTAL OWNER'S EQUITY		**6 600**

9(d)

Non-current assets = £2400 + £1200 = £3600
Depreciation at 10% = 10% of £3600 = £360
Net profit is therefore reduced by £360.
Revised net profit = £5880 – £360 = £5520

10(a)

$$\text{Break-even point} = \frac{\text{fixed costs}}{\text{contribution per unit}}$$

$$1250 = \frac{\text{fixed costs}}{£5 - £2}$$

$$1250 = \frac{\text{fixed costs}}{£3}$$

$$1250 \times £3 = \text{fixed costs}$$
$$\text{fixed costs} = £3750$$

10(b)

Margin-of-safety units = 22% of 1250 = 275

11 Individual responses. Your answer should show accurate and thorough knowledge and understanding of relevant information using specialist technical language, with a well-developed, balanced and logical discussion giving pros and cons.

Points may include some of the following, for example:

- Assets are resources owned by a business and which influence the value of a business. Assets are identified in a business's statement of financial position along with its liabilities and capital (equity).
- Assets are traditionally divided into non-current assets such as machinery and property and current assets such as cash and inventory. These assets are tangible, physical resources.
- Intangible assets are a different category of assets that can be an important influence on the value of a business, such as patents, trade secrets (for example secret formulas), customer databases, copyrights and trademarks.
- Intangible assets can create a competitive advantage over its business rivals and therefore increase its value. Intangible assets are recorded at their cost not their market value. For example, the logo of an American corporation may be worth billions of dollars, but it may have cost less than $100 to create.
- Should a business be sold or taken over by another business, intangible assets may not always be shown on the statement of financial position but they will be taken into account when valuing the business if it is to be sold to another business.
- Intangible assets are sometimes difficult to value and can give a distorted impression when it comes to the value of the business.
- Goodwill is an intangible asset and in some businesses can be one of their biggest assets when it comes to the value of the business.

12 Individual responses. Your answer should show accurate and thorough knowledge and understanding of relevant information using specialist technical language. The balanced analysis should contain linkages and interrelationships between factors, showing logical reasoning.

Points may include some of the following, for example:

- Fixed costs, such as rent, do not vary with output and have to be paid regardless of the level of business activity, whereas variable costs, such as hourly paid employees, vary directly with output. So, if output increases then so will variable costs and vice versa. Semi-variable costs are a combination of fixed and variable costs, such as an annual maintenance contract including a variable element for the number of call-outs per year.
- Fixed costs and variable costs (along with total revenue) are the basis of break-even analysis, which enables the business to make decisions regarding the level of sales which will allow it to break even. After this level of sales has been achieved the business will start to make a profit.
- The basis of those business decisions based upon the notion of the break-even point is the idea of contribution, in other words how much each sale contributes to fixed costs and the required profit level. Contribution can be calculated either as a total contribution or a contribution per unit (selling price per unit – variable cost per unit).
- A business will seek to implement business decisions which maximise this contribution by putting into place business practices which reduce the variable cost per unit. For example, the business may seek to secure cheaper supplies of raw materials. If the contribution per unit can be reduced the break-even point will be lowered which means that the business will have to generate fewer sales before it starts to make a profit.
- An understanding of its cost structure will also allow a business to make a decision on an appropriate margin of safety, in other words the difference between its planned level of sales and the break-even point. This margin of safety allows the business a 'buffer' between its planned sales and the break-even point.
- If semi-variable costs are involved then the variable cost element will also have to be taken into account when calculating the level of contribution.
- Understanding the cost structure of a business is therefore an important factor in the decision-making process within a business in relation to output, sales and price.

13 Individual responses. Your answer should show accurate and thorough knowledge and understanding of relevant information using specialist technical language, with a well-developed, logical, balanced assessment that links and leads to a rational judgement.

Points may include some of the following, for example:

- Acquiring business premises by way of renting or purchase is a major business decision that commits a significant proportion of the business's resources over a long period of time. Both methods involve contractual arrangements which provide the basis of an assessment of their relative advantages and disadvantages.

Renting

- Renting does not result in an increase in the business's non-current assets because the business does not own the premises. The owner of the business commits to paying regular rental payments to the owner of the property (the landlord or their agents).
- Rental payments are likely to remain fixed during the period of the rental agreement.
- As the regular rental payments are likely to be fixed over the medium term, cash flow can be more easily managed as the rent can be regarded as a fixed cost.
- However, the business owner is required to maintain the property in good order, although major repairs will be the responsibility of the owner of the property.
- As the premises are not owned by the business, any increase in the value of the premises will not impact on the value of the business.
- Rent may be subject to on-going reviews at the end of the rental agreement, which could lead to an increase in rent.

Purchasing

- Purchasing business premises may require the owner of the business to secure a commercial mortgage, essentially a long-term business loan that may be repayable in excess of 25 years. The mortgage is subject to interest payments which can be either fixed or variable during all or part of the mortgage repayment period.
- The owner has more flexibility in adapting the premises to meet the needs of the business than a rental agreement, for example redesigning the interior.
- May be able to rent out part of the premises or convert part of the premises into residential accommodation.
- The value of the property may increase over time, depending upon market conditions.
- Purchasing business property increases the value of the business's non-current assets.
- However, depending upon market conditions, the market value of the property may fall.
- Unlike renting, the owner of the business is directly responsible for all costs relating to the upkeep, repair and maintenance of the building.
- A mortgage increases the value of non-current liabilities on the business's statement of financial position which may impact on its ability to secure further business finance.
- If the mortgage involves a variable rate of interest, the owner of the business may not be able to plan cash flow as accurately as with renting since a volatile interest rate market could lead to an increase (but also decrease) in mortgage repayments.

Conclusion

For a new business start-up subject to a high level of risk of failure, a mortgage would not be suitable (and, in any event, it may not be possible for the business owner to secure a mortgage because of the risk of failure). Hence, renting commercial premises is advised for newer businesses. For an established, successful business, purchasing commercial premises may be a suitable option to consider, particularly if the commercial property market is experiencing increasing prices over time.

14 Individual responses. Your answer should show accurate and thorough knowledge and understanding of relevant information using specialist technical language. The well-developed, balanced evaluation should draw on linkages and interrelationships between the factors with a grasp of competing arguments and logical reasoning leading to supported conclusions.

Points may include some of the following, for example:

- **Liquid capital ratio:** this is a measure of Vanessa's business's liquidity, in other words the ability of the business to meet its current liabilities. It does not include inventory so it is a more accurate picture of liquidity. The previous year's figure was worrying because the business only had just over £1 of current assets (discounting inventory) to meet every £1 of its current liabilities. In the current year the business's liquidity has improved and the respective figure is nearly £2 for every £1 of current liabilities
- **Trade receivable days:** the average number of days trade receivables take to pay their invoices. Trade receivable days have increased from 27 days to 32 days. This is a cause of concern since it means invoices are taking longer to be paid, which could result in cash flow problems for Vanessa's business. Tighter credit controls might improve the situation.
- **Inventory turnover:** inventory turnover has gone down from 21 days to 15 days, meaning that there is a greater turnover in the inventory. This could be a positive sign that the business is doing well and selling their stock on a regular basis. However, it could mean that there are shortages of stock (and the need to constantly re-order), which increases the possibility of lost sales.
- **ROCE:** return on capital employed in the current year is greater than in the previous year (8% compared with 6%), which shows that Vanessa is making a bigger return on her investment.
- **Conclusion:** overall, both the business liquidity and ROCE have improved, but trade receivables days have also increased, which is not a good sign of effective credit control. Further investigation would be required to evaluate whether the reduction in her inventory turnover is due to improved business performance in respect of sales.

Practice assessment 4

SECTION A: Personal Finance

1 **Two** of the following:

- rate of interest
- level of inflation
- taxation rates on interest earned.

2 Individual responses. For example, **one** of the following points:

- Used to purchase non-current assets such as machinery, where the business owner pays a deposit with interest charged on the balance remaining.
- The interest rate is fixed over the period of the agreement and payments are made on a regular basis, for example monthly.
- The individual only owns the goods once all the instalments have been made and goods can be repossessed if the individual defaults.

3 Individual responses. Points may include **two** of the below, for example:

- Debt counsellors are specialist agencies or individuals who provide financial advice to individuals who are struggling with personal debt.
- Debt counsellors help an individual prepare a personal budget to help them manage their finances.
- Debt counsellors may contact organisations that are owed money by the individual to agree a repayment plan on behalf of an individual.

4 Individual responses. Your answer should show accurate and thorough knowledge and understanding of relevant information using specialist technical language, with a well-developed, balanced and logical discussion.

Points may include some of the following, for example:

A young adult:

- is likely to have recently entered employment and will be at the first stage in their career
- is likely to be on relatively low earnings, without many surplus funds to enable them to spend
- may want to prioritise an active (and potentially expensive) social life at the expense of putting aside funds for savings
- may not be experienced in budgeting, resulting in high levels of personal debt through credit card and store cards, with the level of their personal debt influenced by marketing campaigns directly aimed at this segment of the market
- may want to own their own home, but struggle to save a deposit and, when they do save, may find that property prices increase at a greater rate than their savings.

A pensioner:

- may also have a limited income, relying on a pension that increases in line with inflation, rather than an income
- may have saved and invested during their working life, which may make the standard of living relatively comfortable
- may not have dependents if their children have left home
- may own their own house, having paid off their mortgage
- may be concerned with their future health and care needs and whether they will have sufficient funds to contribute to their personal health care costs.

5 Individual responses. Your answer should show accurate and thorough knowledge and understanding of relevant information using specialist technical language, with a well-developed, logical, balanced assessment that links and leads to a rational judgement.

Points may include some of the following, for example:

- The main differences between a variable rate instant access account and a fixed interest bond relate to interest rates, access to the funds and the level of risk.

Variable rate instant access savings account:

- the rate of interest can change over time and can increase or decrease
- funds are available 'on demand' by the saver
- the saver is free to deposit funds whenever they have surplus funds available
- the saver may withdraw funds whenever they wish to do so
- the account is convenient, with a small element of risk that the interest rate may fall over time – if this is the case, the account holder may decide to withdraw funds and transfer them to a savings account with another provider paying a higher rate of interest.

Fixed interest corporate bond:

- is issued by a company and is essentially a business loan to the company
- pays a fixed rate of interest
- the interest rate could be higher than that offered by a variable rate savings account, however if interest rates rise, the rate of interest on a bond will remain fixed
- main risk is that, as one of the company's creditors, if the company goes out of business, the investor may not get back all the money they invested, which may deter some from buying corporate bonds.

Conclusion: weighing up both products, the variable rate instant access savings account is a more suitable product for Sarah. She can add further funds into the savings account and, as soon as she has passed her test, she can gain immediate access to her money with which to purchase the car.

6 Individual responses. Your answer should show accurate and thorough knowledge and understanding of relevant information using specialist technical language. The well-developed, balanced evaluation should draw on linkages and interrelationships between the factors with a grasp of competing arguments and logical reasoning leading to supported conclusions.

You should have established the following relevant information to inform your evaluation.

Personal circumstances

- Student (not in regular employment) plays guitar and keyboard in local bars in spare time.
- Charges £30 per evening; performs one or two evenings per week.
- Wishes to upgrade musical equipment following good performance reviews to build bookings and increase booking fee.

Financial circumstances

- Equipment costs £2000 (£700 + £1300).
- Current weekly income £30–£60 per week (variable).
- Savings £200 – requires another £400 to pay for the business studies field trip.
- Overdraft (a personal debt) of £100 (interest free).
- Can extend existing overdraft by another £400 (interest free).

You could use the sentence starters in the hint box on page 64 as you evaluate and link the above and below points.

Points may include some of the following, for example:

- Ferris Bank: could access another £500 of free credit (the overdraft) but interest charges are high once this has been exceeded (24.5%). It is also unwise to start to open up a series of bank accounts to obtain interest free overdrafts since this is risky and may affect his credit history in the future.
- Dialup Credit Ltd: £400 deposit required on the equipment (20% of £2000); could obtain this by extending his existing overdraft to £500 or by using his existing savings (this may not be wise as this would mean that he would have to save another £600 for the field trip); amount of hire purchase required = £2000 – £400 = £1600.

This would need to be repaid in one year which, even without interest payments, would amount to £133.33 per month (£1600/12). This would be risky since his only income is from bookings that are irregular and not guaranteed.

- Clynedale Bank: he would receive £60 in cashback (3% of £2000) but the credit limit is for the full amount of the equipment and with a high rate of interest (24.5%). He would be unwise to make any further payments on the credit card (even though he would receive cashback) because he would reach his credit limit very quickly and so this isn't a bonus for him in the long-term if he only repays the minimum amount owing each month.
- Capo Musical Instruments Ltd: store card is similar in operation to a credit card; he would receive a £200 discount on the equipment (10% of £2000) and the rate of interest at 21.5% is lower than on the credit card, making the store card a better choice than the credit card.
- On balance, the store card might be his best option because he does not need a deposit; he would obtain a discount on the equipment; he could budget for small minimum payments and pay off more if his income increases; he can retain his existing savings for his business studies field trip. However, he should be advised that taking out loans and credit cards without a regular income source is extremely risky.

SECTION B: Business Finance

7 **Two** of the following, for example:
- recording of transactions
- management of business
- compliance with statutory returns
- measuring performance
- controlling, for example trade receivables and trade payables.

8 **Two** of the following, for example:
- bank loan
- debt factoring
- venture capital
- crowd-funding
- loans
- hire purchase
- leasing
- invoice discounting
- trade credit
- grants
- donations
- owner's capital.

9(a)

Cash paid to trade payables = £12 500 + (£18 000 – £13 600)
= £12 500 + £4400
= £16 900

Show your workings for each stage of your calculations as marks may be given for correct workings even if the answer is incorrect.

9(b)

$$\text{Trade receivable days} = \frac{\text{trade receivables}}{\text{credit sales}} \times 365$$

$$= \frac{4600}{87\,500} \times 365$$

= 19.18 days

$$\text{Trade payable days} = \frac{\text{trade payables}}{\text{credit purchases}} \times 365$$

$$= \frac{11\,200}{75\,980} \times 365$$

= 53.8 days

9(c)

Sales		**£180 000**
Cost of sales Opening inventory *Plus* purchases *Less* closing inventory	 £17 000 £105 250 £18 000	 £104 250
Gross profit		**£75 750**
Expenses Rent Insurance Electricity Depreciation	 £8 400 £1 880 £1 920 £2 200	 £14 400
Net profit		**£61 350**

9(d)

Electricity – £525
Insurance + £375 (prepayment)
Revised net profit = £61 350 – £525 + £375 = £61 200

10(a)

Net profit = £61 200
Capital employed = owner's capital + net profit – drawings
= £25 000 + £61 200 – £30 000
= £56 200

$$\text{ROCE} = \frac{\text{net profit}}{\text{capital employed}} \times 100$$

$$= \frac{61\,200}{56\,200} \times 100$$

= 108.89%

10(b)

$$\text{Inventory turnover} = \frac{\text{average inventory}}{\text{cost of sales}} \times 365$$

$$= \frac{(17\,000 + 18\,000)/2}{17\,000 + 105\,250 - 18\,000} \times 365$$

$$= \frac{17\,500}{104\,250} \times 365$$

= 61.27 days

11 Individual responses. Your answer should show accurate and thorough knowledge and understanding of relevant information using specialist technical language, with a well-developed, balanced and logical discussion giving pros and cons.

Points may include some of the following, for example:
- Cash flow difficulties can be a serious problem for businesses such as Ahmed's because it means that their sales revenue is not sufficient to pay their short-term financial liabilities. In Ahmed's case this may mean he is unable to pay his suppliers and may struggle to obtain future supplies.
- Selling non-current assets, particularly if they are not used or are outdated, is a useful short-term solution to generate cash and alleviate cash flow problems.
- However, non-current assets are recorded on a business's statement of financial position and include such things as property, machinery and motor vehicles, so the value of his non-current assets will be reduced. As part of the business's asset structure, along with its current assets, non-current assets influence the value of a business.
- If the non-current assets are a vital part of his business, which are required when repairing computers, he may have to turn away some customers if their computers require more specialist equipment (which he has now sold). As a result, his cash flow problems may increase over time despite the 'short-term fix'.
- He should therefore consider additional ways of addressing his cash flow problems, such as ensuring his customers pay their bills on time and reviewing his current suppliers with regards to their prices and trade credit terms. Most importantly, he should consider ways in which to improve cash inflows from computer repairs and sales.
- **Conclusion:** If Ahmed sells some of the business's non-current assets it is, in effect, a short-term fix because it can reduce the value of the business and, at the same time, result in financial difficulties in the future. For example, productive capacity may be lost due to selling a piece of equipment. He should consider a range of business solutions when addressing cash flow difficulties.

12 Individual responses. Your answer should show accurate and thorough knowledge and understanding of relevant information using specialist technical language. The balanced analysis should contain linkages and interrelationships between factors, showing logical reasoning.

Points may include some of the following, for example:

Contributions

- A carefully prepared cash flow forecast can be an important part of a business's 'management and control toolbox', allowing the business to plan, control and monitor its business operations.
- A cash flow forecast will enable the business to predict when they might have cash flow difficulties, in other words when there is a net cash outflow from the business.
- Identifying potential cash flow problems will enable the business to plan contingency actions to address such cash flow difficulties.
- Monitoring the cash flow forecast will enable the business to set SMART targets for both sales and costs, which can be communicated to managers and the workforce.
- Monitoring targets will also enable the business to identify if there are any weaknesses in its control systems so that management intervention can be implemented. For example, the level of cash sales may be reduced as a result of an increase in credit sales. This will impact on the figures in the cash flow forecast and therefore needs to be planned and controlled to ensure that trade receivables are subject to strict credit control systems.
- Effective management and control systems will be viewed favourably by banks if the business needs to extend its overdraft facilities or apply for a business loan.

Limitations

Ahmed may not be convinced of the usefulness of a cash flow forecast because he considers:

- they are not always accurate
- they may be based upon optimistic assumptions, particularly in respect of sales forecasts
- they may not take into account that costs may rise in the future due to unforeseen circumstances.

Conclusion

Drawbacks are valid but should not detract from the value of such forecasts as part of an overall management monitoring and control system.

13 Individual responses. Your answer should show accurate and thorough knowledge and understanding of relevant information using specialist technical language, with a well-developed, logical, balanced assessment that links and leads to a rational judgement.

Points may include some of the following, for example:

Overview of information in a statement of financial position

- A statement of financial position provides information on what a business owns (its assets) and what it owes (its liabilities) at a specific point in time.
- Assets are classified as non-current (such as equipment, property and machinery) and current assets (such as cash, inventory and trade receivables).
- Liabilities are also classified in the same way – current liabilities are liabilities payable within a 12 month period (such as trade payables) and non-current liabilities which are due after more than a year (such as a medium-term bank loan or a long-term business mortgage).
- The statement of financial position will also include a section on the amount of capital invested by the owners and the profit made in the accounting period, usually one year (minus any drawings made by the owner of the business).

How *Surf the Web*'s statement of financial position could help Ahmed's decision

- Ahmed could use the statement of financial position to calculate the business's liquidity position, its efficiency and the return on investment using ratio analysis.
- Liquidity can be assessed using the current ratio and the liquid capital ratio. Both of these ratios can be used to monitor the business's ability to meet its current liabilities. The liquid capital ratio is a more accurate reflection of liquidity since it excludes inventory.
- Efficiency concerns how well the business is managed and controlled. For example, inventory turnover can be measured using the information in the statement of financial position. This provides an indication if the inventory is being turned around on a regular basis. Holding a large inventory ties up a business's resources whereas a high inventory turnover could be an indication that the business is not always able to meet the requirements of its customers.
- The statement of financial position can be used to calculate the return on capital employed (ROCE) to assess how efficiently the business uses the capital invested in it to generate a return in the form of profit.
- The statement of financial position can also be used to calculate the business's current ratio and liquid capital ratio – in other words whether the business has sufficient current assets to cover its short-term liabilities.

Conclusion

The statement of financial position is one of a number of important pieces of financial information which should be used by Ahmed to assess the financial status of *Surf the Web*. He should also be advised to obtain industry benchmark figures for similar businesses and consider *Surf the Web*'s statement of comprehensive income, looking at the last three years of financial results to identify trends in business performance.

14 Individual responses. Your answer should show accurate and thorough knowledge and understanding of relevant information using specialist technical language. The well-developed, balanced evaluation should draw on linkages and interrelationships between the factors with a grasp of competing arguments and logical reasoning leading to supported conclusions.

Points may include some of the following, for example:

- **Gross profit margin:** This measures the amount of gross profit generated for each £1 of sales. The figures show that Ahmed's business is generating 22p in gross profit for every £1 in sales.
- **Net profit margin:** This measures the amount of net profit generated for each £1 of sales. The figures show that Ahmed's business is only generating 8p in net profit for every £1 in sales. This figure is low particularly as there is not a high volume of sales. Since net profit takes account of business expenses, Ahmed should seriously consider undertaking a review of his business expenses as, if they can be reduced, his net profit margin will rise.
- **Inventory turnover**: Inventory turnover is low, with inventory only being replenished every 91 days (four times a year). This would seem to indicate poor inventory control, with too great a proportion of the business's current assets being tied up in stock. This can result in higher costs such as wastage and pilfering. It is advisable for Ahmed to look at his inventory management systems since this may be one way costs can be reduced.
- **Limitations of ratio analysis**:
  - Based on averages – may hide the fact that one part of the business is performing better than another.
  - Data may have changed since the financial statements were prepared.
  - May be difficult to compare performance with another business if accounting practices are different, for example different rates of depreciation may be used in different businesses.
  - Poor performance may be a reflection of market conditions. For example, an 8% net profit margin may be the average in the industry.
  - Ratios highlight problems but don't provide solutions.
- **Conclusion**

  Ratios are useful indicators and a good starting point for reviewing a business's performance and its financial strength and viability, as well as identifying any potential problems. However, they should be used in conjunction with other financial data to provide a more in-depth picture of a business.

Notes

Notes

Notes